Advance .

Everyone is a Change Agent

"It's often a misconception that change is negative and you need authority to be a change agent. In this book, all those rules are thrown out the window; anyone can create a positive change to advance their community, company, and world! I can really relate to the real-life examples."

-Jessica Rannow, FY17 President, Society of Women Engineers, and Engineering Project Manager

"This book is an excellent reminder to all of us that the target of change should be what and how we do things, not individuals or groups, and that change starts with oneself."

-Edgar H. Schein, Professor Emeritus, MIT Sloan School of Management, and author of *Humble Inquiry* (2013) and *Humble Consulting* (2016)

"*Everyone is a Change Agent* is a refreshing look at how anyone can influence change at work, at home, and in their community. April Mills' key distinction between driving people and driving change is a crucial concept that every change agent must understand and master."

-Heather Stagl, Founder and Change Facilitator at Enclaria

"A powerful, practical 'call to arms' for making real, lasting improvements in your organization and in your life—if you're looking for a common sense approach that you can take charge of, this book is for you."

-Mike Hannan, CEO, Fortezza Consulting

"You will be much more successful at making things better when you understand the difference between driving people and driving change. The first creates resistance; the second invites and engages. Be effective; read this book."

-Gifford Pinchot III, Chairman, Pinchot & Company, and author of *Intrapraneuring — Why You Don't Have to Leave the Corporation to Become an Entrepreneur*

"April makes the principles and practices of change agentry accessible to those who may have been intimidated by it before. She provides key insights into and gently adjusts common (and unhelpful) practices rampant in change initiatives today. Novice change agents and experienced transition managers can learn from this little book."

-Jean Richardson, Principal, Azure Gate Consulting

"The greatest barrier to change is our own minds making us believe that change can't happen. April Mills dissolves the excuses, challenges our assumptions and provides a sober, yet possible path forward to change."

-William Noonan, Author of *Discussing the Undiscussable: A Guide to Overcoming Defensive Routines in the Workplace*

"April did a brilliant job of applying and blending different techniques and methods to create this guide. Everyone is a Change Agent is full of examples and tactics that will allow you to start your change right away. You'll feel inspired by April's passion about change when reading this book."

-Gabriela Simone, Global Agile Coach & Change Agent

Everyone is a Change Agent

• • •

Everyone is a Change Agent

A Guide to the Change Agent Essentials

Keep driving change!
Thank you for all you've
done for me and my
son, Ted.
April K. Mills

April K. Mills

Illustrated by Sarah Moyle

Published by
Engine for Change Press
Cornelius, Oregon
contact@engine-for-change.com

ISBN: 0692772146
ISBN-13: 9780692772140

BUSINESS & ECONOMICS/Leadership

DEDICATION

This book is dedicated to all my fellow change agents,
those of you I've met and those of you I've yet to meet.
Let's change the world together.

FOREWORD

We've all been there: In a meeting listening to an executive exhorting, coaxing, cajoling and pleading for us to get "on board" with the latest change initiative, put our petty skepticism aside and support the program. Usually the more strident the call, the less thoughtful the change. Well-intentioned or not, our first instinct is to question the value of the proposed change and wonder why none of "us" were asked what we thought about the idea.

Posters are printed.

Articles are written.

Emails are sent.

Speeches are given.

And yet ... change doesn't happen.

And we are unfulfilled.

What's wrong?

The answer is in this book: *Everyone is a Change Agent*.

We wave away failure to change with comfortable and common phrases like "well, people just don't like change." Actually, people don't mind change. How else could we explain the concept of progress? The ability to imagine what could be, how things could be better, the difference between the as-is and the to-be state — this is what separates humans from animals. Imagining a better world is an essential ingredient of what makes us human. How could we not like progress then? How could we not like change? It seems we were designed with the concept baked in.

What people don't like is "being changed." We don't like being told what to do, being forced to adapt to a new program, being ordered to do something that is supposedly better for us. It is exactly this truth that April Mills elucidates.

I like to replace the word "change" with "progress" and see what happens. Change is a noun and a verb, so one might try and "change people." But progress is only a noun, you can't really "progress people" (much as some would try), but collectively we can make progress.

Why I love this book:

First, it's intellectually correct and coherent. It clearly contrasts the status quo from what April suggests is a better way. My experience tells me that it is spot on. Instead of driving people, we should drive change. There's a sober approach to the challenges and speed bumps we are likely to encounter.

Second, the book is practical with its seven Change Agent Essentials, recommendations for change agents, augmented with a clearly identified set of eleven tactics. The combination gives us a sensible place to start and a practical roadmap to follow.

Third, it's written and illustrated in an accessible and unpretentious way. Even when the engineer in April shines though, as when she uses algebraic equations to illuminate the structure of her stories, it's not to confuse but to clarify. Note: As a fellow engineer, I'm particularly sympathetic.

Change is a ubiquitous aspect of life and leading change is an essential part of leadership. Every leader is a change agent. At the end of the day, the only person we can control is our self. Attempts to control others always result in manipulation, bad feelings and a sense of being let down. It's a convenient way to dodge responsibility, but it's a lazy cop-out. I personally believe we can't change others, and even changing ourselves is difficult – but possible.

Let's start there…and change the world.

What will our approach be?

I can't do it all, so I will do nothing.

or

I can't do it all, but I can start on something.

I grew up in Concord, Massachusetts, a few miles from where Henry David Thoreau lived during his two years, two months, and two days at Walden Pond. His woodsy observations of human life punctuated my childhood education. April has selected his quote to open the book and I approve. So let's not prune the branches of evil but strike at its root.

L. David Marquet
Author, *Turn the Ship Around!*

CONTENTS

THE SEVEN CHANGE AGENT ESSENTIALS

CHANGE AGENT TACTICS

ACKNOWLEDGMENTS

Thanks to Bob Steinmetz for always asking, "When are you going to write your book?" and believing in me before I entirely believed in myself.

Thanks to the people of the Nuclear Engineering and Planning Department at Puget Sound Naval Shipyard & Intermediate Maintenance Facility (PSNS & IMF) who suffered (not always in silence) my first, poor attempts at change. I remain grateful and apologetic.

Thanks to the hundreds of members of the PSNS & IMF Guiding Coalition teams who partnered with me to try, learn, and achieve so much together. Thanks to Dennis Goin for showing me how to make a Guiding Coalition work—and to Dr. John Kotter for giving us the Guiding Coalition's eight-step change path and continuing to encourage me in my change leadership journey.

Thanks to Rebekah Uhtoff and all the change agents of Bremerton Beyond Accessible Play and the Bremerton community for the joy of our journey that changed lives, just as we hoped. Our amazing change story—and the playground we created where *all* can play—are proof beyond measure that the Change Agent Essentials work.

Thanks to my dear friends who reviewed drafts of this book: Joe Bradley, Julia Bulacio, Colette Berna, Roxanne Bryson, Scott Button,

Adam Cetnerowski, Mike Doyle, Rolf Goetz, Steve Holt, Jay Johnson, Danuta Łuczak-Wieczorek, Giuseppe Miccoli, Matt Mills, Lesley Artyn Nolan, Rae Anne Randall, Jean Richardson, Hilbert Robinson, Andrea Shapiro, Gabriela Simone, Rhea Stadick, Rebekah Uhtoff, Mike Wellborn and Sunny Wheeler.

Thanks to my copy editor, Maureen Hannan, for helping me share my thoughts free of worry of grammar goofs and silly typos.

Thanks to my friend Mike Hannan for investing his time to teach me the ins and outs of self-publishing. Similar thanks to Dr. Dan Diamond for sharing his publishing journey best practices too.

Thanks to my husband and four wonderful kids for supporting me as I live my passion for sharing the Change Agent Essentials with change agents around the world. Hopefully this book answers the question, "What does Mom do?"

Thanks to you, the reader I've been longing to meet for years, for choosing to invest your time in reading this book. It's my honor to write it and share it with you. I look forward to seeing you and your changes succeed now and in the years to come.

April K. Mills
april@engine-for-change.com
everyoneisachangeagent.com
engine-for-change.com
Cornelius, Oregon
August 18, 2016

INTRODUCTION

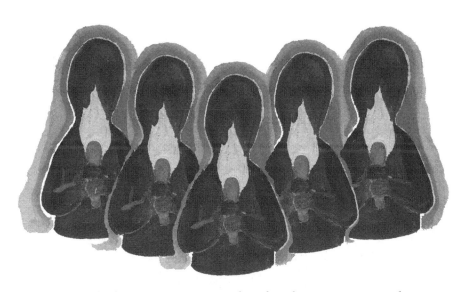

"Leadership is not some mystical quality that some possess and others do not. As humans, we all have what it takes...."

— L. DAVID MARQUET

A change agent is someone who acts to create the changes they want to see around them. Everyone is a change agent.

A change is a difference you are determined to make, whether as an individual or as part of a group or organization. *Change*—a name I prefer to more commonly used terms like "project" or "initiative"—is any effort undertaken with the goal of innovating a solution, meeting a need, or otherwise improving the world. It is the delta between what is and what you imagine could be. A change is, however simple or complex, your effort to make the world a better place.

Is there a change you want to see in your life, work, community, or nation? Is there a change you want to make in the world?

Have you been waiting for someone, somewhere, to create your change? You don't have to wait. You can start today.

Perhaps you've already tried to create the change you want to see, but you've struggled or failed. If so, you're not alone.

This book is, as the title suggests, for *everyone*. There are particular changes you want to see. Whether you've been successful or not in the past, studying and applying this *Guide to the Change Agent Essentials* will help you implement your changes faster and more easily. And, I believe, with a great deal more joy.

The journey to create a change is much like setting out on a hike into new territory. You know others have been here before, because you can see the trails they've blazed. Yet, when the route forks, you're uncertain which route is best. It is into this confusion that I offer my services.

I would be honored to be your guide on your change journey. Like a mountain guide, I've gone before you to study the maps left by change pioneers. I've tested the terrain, designed custom tools to guide our journey, and cleared many of the obstacles that often block the path to the summit. I have a passion for helping people achieve the changes they desire. I'm grateful to be on your journey with you.

This journey includes four parts: Discovery, Planning, Acting, and Leading. Within these four parts, I'll share seven Change Agent Essentials that successful change agents use. The **Change Agent Essentials** are recommendations for action based on experience and results in similar situations. You can use them too—today!

This is a deeply personal book for me, filled with stories I've lived, people I love, and heroes I look to for inspiration. The stories fall into two categories: generic and personal.

For the generic stories, I'm using a concept I call **Change Algebra,** descriptions of change stories using variables to substitute for specific people, changes, and organizations.

Person X, who works for Organization Y, encountered Obstacle A when creating Change B.

Change Algebra is useful for three reasons.

First, Change Algebra highlights the universal characteristics of the Change Agent Essentials.

Person X may be anyone.

Organization Y could be a public, private, or nonprofit establishment.

Obstacle A is a challenge relating to budget, time, scope, or rule(s).

Change B might be any desired change to a process, behavior, or culture.

The particulars of the story matter much less than the methods. What is most significant is *how* Person X discovers, plans for, acts on, and leads the change they seek.

Second, Change Algebra—because it reduces stories of change to their simplest terms—will help you rapidly translate the essentials back into your own context.

When I teach classes on the Change Agent Essentials, students often ask for stories directly relevant to their individual environments. These stories are easy enough to provide when I'm speaking to a limited group of people within a specific organization. However, as the audience size increases, the examples can become tedious and distracting. To include a story for everyone in this book would mean burying the essentials in mountains of unnecessary detail.

Change Algebra clears away all distracting detail, allowing you to imagine yourself in the story. As you insert your own X, Y, A, and B into the anecdotes in this book, you'll see your specific work experience come to life, as if illustrated in the panels of a popular business cartoon.

Third, Change Algebra protects the identities of the people and organizations in my change stories.

It can be challenging (or even impossible) to get permission to use story specifics from the officials deputized to protect them. Hence, Change Algebra overcomes the permission obstacle by eliminating specifics while preserving the core of the story. Even better, many people who were close to the stories will likely think I am telling one story when I'm actually telling another. This further proves the universal aspects of these essentials.

For the personal stories, I've included episodes that have transformed me as a change agent, in the hopes that they'll lead you to your own transformative breakthroughs. These are stories of both failures and successes from my personal life, professional experience, consulting practice, and community efforts.

A story we'll return to often throughout the book is about how an amazing group of citizens and I formed Bremerton Beyond Accessible Play, building the first accessible playground in our region for children and adults with special needs. I'll refer to it here, as we often did, simply as "the playground project." It was a full implementation of the seven Change Agent Essentials, and I'll use it to illustrate the essentials in action.

For me, the playground project was a change agent's dream turned reality. I've written *Everyone is a Change Agent* in the hopes that the playground project, along with the Change Agent Essentials that enabled it, will equip and encourage you to reach your own change dreams.

As in any guide, we will require some custom terms to make sense of our journey. Throughout the book you'll find terms marked in **bold** when they are defined. Their definitions are also included in the glossary at the end of the book.

At the end of *Everyone is a Change Agent* you'll also find two Change Agent Action Templates to help you quickly begin your change (or improve your ongoing changes). You'll also find suggested readings to continue your change journey until we meet again—as well as a brief list of references.

As this book is a manual, I've intentionally stated facts directly, without citations and footnotes, to keep the discussion brief and practical. If you are looking for a deeply cited synthesis of the research and literature that underpins the Change Agent Essentials, watch for one of my future books or contact me at april@engine-for-change.com.

I'm honored to be your guide on this change agent journey. Let's begin.

Part 1

DISCOVERY

*"The place to improve the world is first in one's own heart and
head and hands, and then to work outward from there."*

— ROBERT PIRSIG

O pportunities for change are all around us.

Some of us spend all our time studying how to make change. Others go about attempting to create it without thinking at all about what they are doing or why they are doing it.

In both cases, most of us fail to achieve the changes we seek in our lives, work, communities, nations, and world. Why?

What can we discover in our common experiences that can guide us toward the successful, joyful changes we want to see in our lives?

What must we know before we can plan, act, and lead the changes we desire?

What are we missing?

Chapter 1

●　●　●

THE STATUS QUO:DRIVING PEOPLE

*"If you think the problem is out there, that
very thought is the problem."*

—— STEPHEN R. COVEY

C hildren learn by mimicking their parents. I know this from experience, both from my own childhood and from being a mother of four young children. Whether my behavior is good or bad, useful toward my goal of a joyful household or not, the children follow my lead. The same learning mechanism, mimicking, affects our work and our community life.

We learn much more about our employer's expectations from our co-workers than we ever do from a new employee indoctrination class. We watch how other citizens engage with government officials and do the same.

FIRST TRY

This pattern of mimicking seems obvious to me now, but eleven years ago, when I was given my first chance to be a project manager, it wasn't obvious at all. I had volunteered for the role of project manager because of my passion for the particular change project—and for the positive impact I knew it could achieve. Some might say I begged for the job—and... they'd be right.

Once I got the job, I couldn't wait to get started. I began my project just as I had seen others begin theirs, with the organizational weapon of choice: the mandatory meeting invite.

I picked the individuals I wanted based on their organizational positions. I crafted a spreadsheet of all the tasks they needed to accomplish and the dates by which they needed to accomplish them. I proudly presented my plan to the mandatory attendees.

I think they attended the first meeting because they were curious. They probably wondered: "Who is this young lady? What authority does she think she has to tell us what to do?"

They arrived at the second meeting to tell me all the ways I was wrong; I hardly listened. I had a mandate from the senior manager to push the project forward, and I thought that was all the authority I needed.

When the third meeting arrived, my mandatory attendees simply didn't show up. I complained about their lack of commitment to the senior manager. He didn't listen. I yelled louder. That approach didn't work either. My change project ground to a halt.

FORCING CHANGE

I was stunned. Though I'd mimicked what I'd seen before, I'd also gone one step further. I had based my plan on a highly regarded eight-step process for change—outlined by John Kotter in his 1996 book, *Leading Change*.

I had, I thought, found the perfect recipe for effective change leadership. I dedicated myself to following the steps perfectly.

Step 1: Establish a Sense of Urgency.

I sent my mandatory meeting notice mere moments after I was appointed project manager. Now that's urgency!

Step 2: Create the Guiding Coalition.

Check! When I sent my mandatory meeting invite, I picked attendees—some might say, conscripts—from various parts of the organization, and I ensured they were senior enough in the hierarchy to get something done. When I say, "get something done," I mean I thought they would use their authority to make more people do what I wanted them to do.

Step 3: Develop a Vision and Strategy.

I had a vision and a strategy, and I intended to make sure they all understood it—in excruciating detail.

My spreadsheet was flawless. It was filled with *their* names, and *my* detailed instructions of what they must do and when they must do it. I assigned my conscripts tasks that stretched out for months ahead and would take several hours each week to be completed well. What could go wrong?

Step 4: Communicate the Change Vision.

I told them my change vision. I told them over and over and over again what they must do in order to make my change happen. I don't think they wanted to hear it, but I didn't ever ask them. I was confident that telling was more important than listening. *Tell. Tell. Tell.*

Later, as a I thought back over that initial failed effort toward change, I realized the attendees tried to tell me what I was doing wrong. But when they did, I either refused to listen or failed to really hear what they were saying. In short, my colleagues' efforts to offer constructive feedback didn't work.

And that is as far as I got.

At this point I could have blamed my colleagues, given up on the change, and found a new role with other people who could understand my vision. I *could have*, but I didn't.

Instead, my engineering training kicked in, and I began to analyze the situation. I felt compelled to figure out why my methods for leading change—methods I understood to be tried and true—were not working. I knew I couldn't troubleshoot the problem until I could name it. After reflecting on my approach, I realized I had been guilty of *driving people.*

Driving people is using some form of coercion (e.g., orders, fear of negative consequences, removal or application of positive consequences) to compel others to change.

Does this picture look anything like change initiatives you've experienced? Have you ever been the conscript who was forced to carry out change? Will you admit to being the one holding the whip? I'll admit it. I'm not proud of it, but if I'm honest, that's exactly what I was doing.

I had borrowed the whip of authority from the senior manager who appointed me. I used that authority to compel the conscripts to make my change happen…"or else!" I did all I could think of to make the threat of *no change* seem worse than the threat of change. Nothing worked.

In the years since that experience, as I've talked with many change agents, I've learned my failed first effort at leading change wasn't unusual. It was, in fact, all too common.

DRIVING PEOPLE IS THE STATUS QUO

Driving people is the status quo. It is the recipe nearly all change agents follow, and we have most often done so without much thought or reflection. Like most recipes, the *driving people template* relies on our mimicking what we see and trusting we'll get results. When we do get the results we seek, we assume our actions—our faithful following of the recipe—generated the success. And when we don't? Most of us will, by reflex, assume the fault lies with others.

Richard Feynman, Nobel Prize-winning physicist and brilliant story-teller, told a similar story is his Caltech Commencement Address in 1974. He introduced the world to the Cargo Cult. I'll summarize the core of the story.

CARGO CULT

During World War II, American service members arrived on a Pacific island to build a supply station. The island was inhabited. When the service members arrived, the islanders watched their actions with a great deal of interest.

The islanders saw the Americans clear some land, build a long flat strip, and signal for something. Then, suddenly, enormous shiny birds glided in from the sky, carrying amazing cargo.

The islanders were intrigued. They wanted these same treasures of cargo from the heavens. They rushed to their part of the island, cleared some land, built a flat strip, and waved flags to signal to the skies. Then, they waited for the large, shining birds to land with their cargo.

No cargo arrived.

The islanders could not learn how to receive cargo merely from observation and assumptions based on past experience. Absent more knowledge, all the islanders could do was mimic as best they could the actions they were able to see. Mimicking the American soldiers would never be enough to get the islanders the cargo they sought.

Absent the cargo, the mystified islanders tried to find a reason for their failure. According to Wikipedia's Cargo Cult entry, they concluded "that the foreigners had some special connection to the deities and ancestors of the natives, who were the only beings powerful enough to produce such riches."

GRATEFUL FOR FAILURE

I'm grateful that I failed to implement my first major change effort. The experience spurred me to re-examine how I go about creating change—and what leads to failure.

First I asked myself, "Was my failure an isolated case or a pattern?" I found a pattern.

Next, I asked myself, "How many important changes have I attempted that failed to achieve their desired results? Too many? A majority?"

Many. Yes, and yes.

Realizing there was a widespread pattern of failure, I searched for a cause or causes. I delved deeper into the whole notion of driving people. If this approach doesn't work in a majority of cases, why would we continue to use it? I found three answers to my question:

First, we keep driving people because we don't admit that it fails.

Second, we keep driving people because we don't count the costs of doing so.

Third, we keep driving people because we don't know what else to do.

ADMITTING FAILURE

In the May-June 1991 *Harvard Business Review* article "Teaching Smart People How to Learn," Chris Argyris explains that successful people encounter failure so rarely that when they do fail, they fear admitting their part in it. He concludes, "They cast blame outward—on anyone or anything they can."

In my experience, Argyris's thesis is most certainly true. Several months ago, a program manager and I were looking at the "driving people" illustration. I was using it to emphasize that in driving people the burden of the change is on the worker bees of the change. The program manager said, "Well, of course it is. That way, if they succeed, I succeed; but if they fail, then only they fail."

Change agents who embrace the "driving people" status quo may believe they'll avoid the consequences of failure, but often I've seen the consequence fall upon the change agent too. There's an election, a reorganization, a retirement or promotion, and poof!—their personal or borrowed authority evaporates. When that upheaval inevitably happens, the weight of the change crushes the people being driven and the change agent too. Deadlines are missed. New approvals must be won. The process begins again.

Now, you shouldn't attempt to avoid this "crush danger" by keeping people in their positions of authority just so they can sustain the force. Death, after all, comes eventually to all authority.

It would, rather, be better never to hang the heavy weight of change above anyone's head. When, inevitably, that weight comes crashing down, it will cause trauma, crippling their ability to learn from the failure. Plus, the crushing weight does (sometimes irreparable) damage to the very change you seek. All of this damage comes with very high costs.

COUNTING THE COSTS

The costs of failed change can be described with three broad cost categories: People, Time, and Results.

PEOPLE COSTS

People Costs are the negative effects of failed changes that people store in their hearts and minds—effects that delay or derail the next change.

When you suggest, "We should implement Process X," or "We should try Policy Y," and the people gasp or cry in pain or anguish, you've found a people cost. They are gasping or crying because you've poked what I call their *change scars*. **Change scars** are the psychological vestiges of bad past change efforts that manifest as physical and emotional reactions to new change.

In some organizations and communities, years of failed changes have wounded and re-wounded people to the point that they recoil physically from mere words. Only after spending days, weeks, or months healing the change scars can the change agent begin the implementation.

Another people cost from failed change is diminished morale and loss of good people. Loss takes two forms: physical departures (the more obvious flight from trauma) and emotional departures. People who have departed emotionally continue to draw a paycheck, attend your meetings, and live in your communities—but they are apathetic or resistant to change. They are numb. You've no doubt known these people or have occasionally been one yourself. You can calculate these costs from your own experience.

TIME COSTS

We all have only 24 hours in each day and seven days in each week. Whether you're the CEO of your company or the newest entry-level employee, you have the same limited number of hours to work with. Given this universal limitation, it is amazing to me how much time is spent continuing to meet over projects that everyone (okay, nearly everyone) knows won't succeed. We can call these change initiatives—these efforts that people continue to revisit long after the life has gone out of them—**Change Corpses.**

When I've shared the "change corpse" term with audiences around the world, laughter erupts from the crowd. This universal laugh tells me that we've all been part of these changes and are living amongst these change corpses today.

So, if these change corpses are universal, the next question is: Why do we keep tending to them?

I have found that people keep attending to the change corpses because they don't know how to bury them without admitting failure. There are many ways to bury them, but I'll share one way that often works for me.

TACTIC: BURY THE CORPSE

When the meeting time arrives to attend to the change corpse, I create an excuse to cancel the meeting—any excuse. Then (and this is the important detail), I cancel the meeting *series*, not just the occurrence.

Then, I wait. I wait for the next regular meeting time to arrive, and I see if anyone mentions the lack of the meeting. If they don't, I know I have successfully buried the corpse.

If someone inquires, I ask them why they are asking. Usually I hear something like, "My boss expects me to attend, so I need to attend or tell my boss it's cancelled." I encourage them simply to tell their boss it is cancelled. I've never had a boss approach me to complain about a cancellation. Corpse buried.

The abundant presence of change corpses has convinced me that the status quo is this: The Time Costs (the meetings, projects, initiatives and community forums held for already failed changes) will accrue until the end of time unless we stage a deliberate intervention.

In the absence of any intervention, the scheduling system default of endlessly recurring meetings demands that we keep caring for the corpses of long-dead endeavors. What if the default was, instead, to pick an end date before launching a recurring series? We would be burdened with far fewer change corpses (and their ongoing costs).

RESULTS COSTS

When changes stall or stop, they are much like cars broken down on the highway. They clog flow for everything and everyone behind them. The clogs prevent new, needed change from getting attention, gaining traction, and moving forward. Thus, failed changes lead to big costs—from time-wasting delays to goals missed altogether.

Think back to a time when you were advocating for a change. Were you told to wait until Change X was accomplished? Did you want to go move Change X to the side (or bury it) to make a lane for your change? I'll bet you did.

When we clean up the road or unclog the pipeline (pick your metaphor) to get change flowing, we'll always get better results.

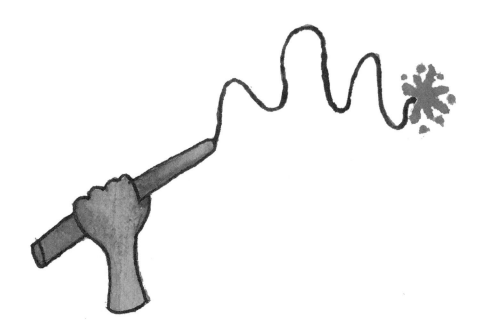

MOVING BEYOND DRIVING PEOPLE

With that failed change I led, the one where I ordered, whipped, tattled, and at least once screamed, I went back and apologized to the people involved. I told them I was sorry for what I had done. I told them I wouldn't do that to them or others again. Then I went searching for a new way.

> *"Finish each day and be done with it...Tomorrow is a*
> *new day. You shall begin it serenely and with too high*
> *a spirit to be encumbered with your old nonsense."*
>
> — RALPH WALDO EMERSON

Let's abandon our old nonsense of driving people and begin our new day.

Chapter 2

● ● ●

THE POWERFUL ALTERNATIVE: DRIVING CHANGE

*"People willing to make changes need first
and foremost to work on themselves."*

—— *JURGEN APPELO*

"There has to be a better way!"

The thought nagged at me. I had to find the better way. I searched the literature, read history, and looked everywhere.

Increase motivation, build trust, be a great leader, create an effective culture; these are all great statements, but they're not enough. They are a *what*, but not a *how*. What was behind them? What comes before motivation, trust, leadership, and culture?

Then one day I realized that a multitude of authors and thinkers have described successful change, yet no one has applied a name and a picture outlining its essential elements. Quickly, a concept and picture snapped into place. I call it **Driving Change**.

Driving Change is choosing a change for yourself, acting to create it, and clearing the obstacles for others to join you and change themselves.

In every story of successful change, you will find a change agent who chose to commit to a change, started working on the change, and cleared the obstacles for others to join them.

The change agent built trust with others by demonstrating their commitment to the change and making it safe for their fellow coworkers, employees, members or citizens to step forward, contribute, and shine.

The change agent focused on the change before them, painted an inspirational picture of the view from atop the summit of success, and blazed the way toward it.

The change agent asked, "Who wants to join me?" Enthusiastic followers raised their hands. The change was off and running.

When a change agent is driving change, they give off a vitality that is contagious. Think back on successful, even joyful, changes you've experienced. Were they based on these core principles of driving change?

DRIVING CHANGE POWERS SUCCESS

My first failure with driving a project using John Kotter's 8-step model from *Leading Change* didn't deter me from trying again. From 2007 to 2013 I was Managing Director of the Commander's Guiding Coalition at Puget Sound Naval Shipyard and Intermediate Maintenance Facility (PSNS&IMF) in Bremerton, Washington.

When we created the Guiding Coalition, we selected people who had volunteered. They wanted the chance to create change and were willing to accept responsibilities on top of their regular day jobs in order to do it. The Guiding Coalition members were new employees, veteran employees, and managers of various levels. What they all had in common was their willingness to adhere to the Guiding Coalition's cardinal rule: *drive change*. And that willingness made all the difference.

In New York in 2011, at the Theory of Constraints International Certification Organization (TOCICO) conference, I was privileged to share the story of the Guiding Coalition's success. Powered by their commitment to driving change, the Guiding Coalition's exceptional members had, by that time, achieved more than 75 successes. The changes varied in size, scope, and focus area but they were consistently created by driving change.

Earlier, in 2010, Professor John Kotter had visited PSNS&IMF to see for himself a successful implementation of his model. On that March day, we held a typical Guiding Coalition meeting, featuring approximately 30 volunteer change agents seated at a large horseshoe-shaped table—with 20 or more senior managers sitting behind them against three of the four conference room walls.

After completing the hour-long biweekly meeting, Dr. Kotter offered a few remarks. He said:

> *"Only 15 percent of all organizations are really trying to understand how to live with and respond to the rate of change. Of the organizations, 15 percent are trying to move in a direction that they know works, 14 of the 15 percent are struggling because of the culture or environment that drives them. Only one percent of the organizations in the world are making progress; they are doing what you all are doing."*

Later that day, at a separate forum, Dr. Kotter said of the Guiding Coalition's successes, "The world needs to see this." I'm grateful that he went on to show the world, in his 2014 book *Accelerate*, some of what we achieved. (Obviously I'm biased, but I highly recommend the book. It is, as the author states in the opening line, "a book about pioneers, for pioneers.")

What we were doing then in 2010, what Kotter wrote about in 2014, and what I'm sharing with you now in this book, are change leadership essentials. If you're looking for the magic that produces amazing results, you must learn the elements of driving change.

DRIVING THE PLAYGROUND CHANGE

When I and the members of Bremerton Beyond Accessible Play started the playground project, we didn't know much about building playgrounds—but we knew about driving change. We made a deliberate decision *not* to take the adversarial approach many frustrated citizens had done before. We would not go stomping into the mayor's office or a city council meeting to demand the city build a playground or else.

Instead, we sought out Parks Director Wyn Birkenthal and asked him to partner with us to build a playground. In that first meeting, I made the appeal, "We want an accessible playground in this city as soon as possible. We are willing to work hard with you to achieve it. How can we partner to create an accessible playground in Bremerton?"

Birkenthal and his staff's landscape architect, Colette Berna, said they could support us through connecting us with the parks commission, the mayor, and the city council. They also offered to lead the grant-writing process. Once we arrived at the building stage, they said, they would also provide parks staff as available.

We community members wanted an accessible playground, and the parks department now wanted it too. But they needed a partner to raise community awareness, campaign for funding, provide design criteria, and coordinate volunteers to build the playground. We promised to be that partner.

We all shook hands and agreed to meet again soon. The playground project had begun. We were now all choosing the change—and we were, together, clearing the obstacles so we could move fast. *That's* the power in driving change.

A NAME FOR WHAT THEY'VE ALWAYS DONE

Throughout time, successful change agents have followed a pattern similar to:

I want Change A. Somebody must create Change A.

I am somebody. I can start today.

Over the years, I've had the great privilege to meet many phenomenal change agents who have been driving change for a long time. Of course, that's not what they and their peers have called it. Some have called it good leadership, or excellent project or program management skills, or just being ourselves.

Only a few weeks ago, I commiserated with a fellow change agent about the way many people have responded to our successes. We laughed sadly as we recalled the number of times we've heard either:

"We wish we could clone you!" or "Well that's just you. You can't expect anyone else to do it too."

These platitudes are sad to remember because of all the wasted potential they represent.

Through these words well-meaning people have blocked others from taking any action or learning anything. The platitudes tell others that change success comes from being the especially talented Person A. So, if I'm Person X, is it hopeless to even try? Left without another option, Person X settles for being a change conscript or returns to driving people too.

This must stop!

Successful change agents who possess the awareness to *define* what they are doing as driving change have immense power. They hold the power to *multiply their influence*, because they can show others how to follow their example.

TRANSFORMED BY DRIVING CHANGE

I've had the privilege to share the concept of driving change with audiences and students around the world. I've watched people across continents and cultures transformed before my eyes from successful change agents labeled "different" or from conscripts struggling under the whips of driving people into capable, confident change agents.

Once they were instructed in driving change, they seized their inherent power and began to create their changes right away. Their change successes are numerous and varied. Their method was the same: driving change.

Chapter 3

● ● ●

THE COMPARISON: DRIVING PEOPLE VS. DRIVING CHANGE

"...[C]hoice exists only (1) when there are at least two possible courses of action available to the decision maker, (2) where there are at least two possible outcomes of unequal value... and (3) when the different courses of action have different effectiveness....Choice exists when the action of the decision maker makes a difference in the value of the outcome."

— RUSSELL ACKOFF

Which path you choose—driving people or driving change—matters more than any other aspect or attribute of your change.

You don't need to take me at my word. I believe your experience will prove to you the truth of this critical dichotomy. Let's examine a basic scenario that most of us have encountered: a change in a process at work.

The goal is to implement Process W. We are currently following Process V. The budget (e.g., time and money) for the change is X. The people in the midst of the change are Person A, Person B, and Group C.

We've set the change, budget, and people as fixed. Now, let's run the change first by driving people, next by driving change—and then compare the results. We'll start with the status quo, driving people.

DRIVING PEOPLE

The first step in driving people is to appoint the person who will drive the others.

Person A is ordered to push the change.

Person A then sends a mandatory meeting notice to Person B and Group C.

In that first meeting Person A tells B and C what they must do and when they must do it. Person A will outline the punishments if Process W isn't followed and the rewards if it is.

Person B and Group C might have concerns but they will often be told to forget those concerns and start doing Process W, or else.

These meetings will happen weekly until the punishments are great enough, the rewards are great enough or the interest in the change evaporates and the effort to implement Process W stops.

Been there?
Now for the alternative.

DRIVING CHANGE

The first step in driving change is to find a person who wants to implement Process W, is willing to go first, and is excited to clear the obstacles for their coworkers to accomplish the change too.

Person A volunteers to drive the implementation of Process W because Person A believes it is a crucial change for the organization's success.

Person A seeks others to volunteer to help with the change. Person A asks Person B and Group C if they want to join.

Person B says yes. Group C says no. Person A thanks them both.

When Person B has concerns, Person A listens—and together they act on the concerns. (This is the removal of obstacles to allow people to move the change forward.)

Now when Person B approaches Group C, armed with the lessons learned trying to implement Process W, it is more likely that

Group C will voluntarily follow Process W or share their concerns and follow soon.

The first win is gaining the support of Person B toward Process W.

The next win is the initial learning Persons A and B gain when they try to implement Process W together.

The last, best win is when Process W is implemented and everyone feels a respected part of the change.

This example may seem over-simplified, but it is very typical of driving change. The ease comes from where the force is applied and what leverage that force gives a change agent.

WHERE IS THE FORCE APPLIED?

Both driving people and driving change, include "driving", a force to propel the change. The similarities end there.

When you're driving people, you're applying the force directly to the people.

Forcing people is time-consuming, because you must first access the people (and their attention) to apply the force. To meet these demands, organizations create project managers, program managers, change managers, and more. When you drive people, the force you apply to them reflects back onto you—and it's exhausting.

I've met harried executives who fly endlessly around the world visiting their employees, forcing the change through their physical presence. This travel comes on top of other efforts via email or teleconference to compel, cajole, and threaten. No matter how much these frazzled executives do, it never seems to be enough. Finally, they resort to multi-day face-to-face meetings, which could sadly be referred to as "driving people galas."

Multi-day face-to-face meetings are held to convince the conscripts that the change is a good one. Sometimes the meeting produces a slight increase in the general level of enthusiasm toward the change. Usually, however, the increase lasts only as long as it takes everyone to drive to the airport to fly home. A few months from now there will be another face-to-face meeting to try again. The cycle is exhausting, expensive, and often futile.

Even when a person is won to a change, they sometimes end up abandoning it a day, or week, or month later. When that happens, it's usually because the pull of the status quo was just too strong, and it's easier to go back to the way things always have been. The organization stagnates. The cycle restarts. Time passes. Nothing changes.

Nothing changes because the force, when applied to people, simply doesn't stick. It slides off faster than food off a non-stick pan. It's a good thing we have another option.

When we are driving change, we are applying the force to the change. This is the higher point of leverage for our change. We focus on the rules we can modify, the budgets we can apply, the obstacles we can remove. These things, once changed, *stay* changed until we change them again.

Freed from chasing people around the world in vain attempts to trigger action, we can (when we are driving change) focus on what we need to change in our own behaviors and how we can remove obstacles to our partners' actions. These are high-leverage acts, because (again), once completed, they stay completed. We are slowly but surely moving toward the change we seek.

When a change agent applies force to their change, they are demonstrating their courage by going first and creatively overcoming obstacles. And they are showing their true leadership by charting a course to the future that others can follow.

Driving change emphasizes another point that is missed by driving people. Driving people keeps the change at a distance. When we're being driven, we say, "It is my boss's change." Or "The city is changing." We don't own it. When we're driving people, we are waiting for briefings, reports, and/or meetings, to learn how the change is progressing.

In contrast, driving change makes the change very personal. The change agent, to drive change, is part of the change, immersed in it, at the front of it. This gives the change agent real-time situational awareness.

When you are driving change, you know where your change stands at all times. It is this real-time situational awareness that allows for rapid response to both negative and positive developments. And it is this awareness that also speeds the change considerably over driving people.

WHICH IMPLEMENTS CHANGE FASTER?

As I've shared this message of driving people and driving change around the world, I've been asked many times, "But isn't it faster to implement change when you're driving people? My answer has been and will always be, "No."

When others suggest that driving people makes change speedier to implement, they are often thinking only of the moment it takes them to issue the order, "Begin." They aren't measuring the time from start to full implementation or even first results; that is much, much longer.

In my experience, when you're driving people, the implementation takes months to produce the first results. Sometimes the first results aren't seen for years. And, often, when you drive people, your change implementation is abandoned before it can produce any results.

Rather than filling with results, the months and years of the implementation fill with meetings and methods to check on the change. And the long stretches in between are stagnant, as everyone waits for the change to happen. The final months, if the change hasn't already become a change corpse, are full of efforts to redesign the change and to reissue the order under a new title.

IMPLEMENTATION BY DRIVING PEOPLE

When you're driving people, you:

Issue order for people to change to Process A.

Wait X months for the order to reach everyone.

Wait X + 12, 24, or 36 months for people to change. You regularly or rarely check for results.

Finding no results or less than the desired results, you issue another order for people to change to Process A. However, you rename it Process B to avoid the change scars created by the failed implementation of Process A.

We can do better.

IMPLEMENTATION BY DRIVING CHANGE

When you're driving change:

You think implementing Process X is the right thing for your organization.

You announce to the people affected by Process X that you intend to begin to implement Process X immediately.

You ask them to please join you or to tell you why they can't or won't.

You listen to their concerns and act on the ones you can. Then you go first and encourage them to go with you.

By the end of that first day, you've gathered a wealth of information about your change. You know who is with you and your proposed change and who can't (or won't) support you and why. You have a list of the obstacles you can work on right away. You may even quickly decide to modify the change or abandon it altogether.

On that first day, you aren't miles down the trail toward your change, but you have made important progress. By comparison, if you had been driving people, you'd still be standing at the trailhead yelling to others to get moving.

DRIVING CHANGE AT HOME

Here's how driving change looks in my home life. I announce to my kids, "I intend to clean the house, and I'd appreciate your help. Is there something you'd most like to do or anything you need from me to get you started?"

The two-year-old stares at me confused but doesn't leave my side.

The four-year-old volunteers to help with everything.

The eight-year-old pretends he didn't hear me.

The 11-year-old says, "I'll clean my room and bathroom," and runs away before I can suggest additions to her list.

Now, through merely declaring my intent, I know which of the children supports, resists, or is neutral to my change. I've found this a much faster start to my "clean the house" change then my old method of declaring "We're all cleaning the house now. Your job is..." That usually cost me at least a half an hour responding to all the objections that my order was unreasonable, ill-timed, or both. Their subsequent lackluster or non-existent progress would then further remind me of the flaw in driving people.

Does this sound like a familiar pattern to you at home, at work, or in your community?

WHICH GIVES THE BEST RETURN ON TIME INVESTED?

Now that we've discussed how driving change is a quicker path to re-sults than driving people, let's look at returns on investment from driving people and driving change.

When you're driving people, there are meetings, meetings, and more meetings. You'll have meetings to discuss who will be conscripted onto the team to force the change. You'll have meetings to plan the change. You'll have meetings within meetings about what the change should really be. (And they'll usually involve lots of statements that start with, "What I think Authority Figure A wants us to do is....")

Oh, the meetings! Where is the action? We discuss, argue, convince, disagree, re-argue, and re-convince (by force or reward this time). Ugh! It's draining.

I call this the "whirlpool effect", because it can feel like your time is draining into a swirling abyss. (You're probably laughing now, unless you're crying. Maybe you're both laughing and crying. Take heart, you're not alone. I'm right there with you.)

There is a better way.

When you are driving change, you are using the time you have—along with the people, budget, and resources you have—to do what you can. In short, you are focused on the present and its potential to create the future.

If you have only three people, then together you plan for what can be done with a team of three people.

If you have only a $10,000 budget, then you focus on maximizing what you can accomplish now with a $10,000 budget. Then, if necessary, you seek out more funding.

If you can move only a step or two forward during each time you meet, then you accept that progress cheerfully—rather than refusing to act until you have a plan that "guarantees" the change results you seek.

Since there are only 24 hours in each day and seven days in each week, we must maximize the return on our investment of time. Consider the value of an hour invested in driving change—with people who believe in the change and are clearing the path for others to join in. That hour will return more results than a week drained into the whirlpool of driving people.

WHICH BUILDS TRUST?

Trust is essential in change. We must build trust, with ourselves, others, organizations, and societies. We do this by choosing trust for ourselves and clearing the obstacles for others to trust too.

In *Speed of Trust,* Stephen Covey provides a compelling example of driving change to build trust. Worried about a lack of trust after a major organizational merger, Covey declared during an important meeting that he wanted to discuss the attendees' lack of trust in him. After the meeting, he writes, "one participant told me that I had established more trust in one day than I had in the past several months." Covey was driving change; and his example demonstrates how powerful this approach is for creating lasting joy and success.

When we're driving change, we are building trust—with ourselves and those around us—because we are living our values, tying values to actions, and opening ourselves up to constructive, obstacle-clearing feedback.

Not everyone will trust you when you are driving change, but I've found that others' willingness to trust has more to do with them than with you. Change scars are deep for some people. Some are used to change by driving people—and driving people is, at its core, based on a lack of trust.

When someone is driving people, they are assuming they cannot trust their colleagues to accept a change without force or rewards. And, rather than working on the change, they spend their time working on methods to coerce or cajole.

If I'm the one being driven, I am reluctant to trust those who are driving me: I've learned through past changes that most punishments are hollow threats and most rewards are false (or overstated) promises.

My heart aches every time I see or experience the fundamental mistrust that exists among teams built upon driving people.

Let me be blunt: If your status quo is driving people, your efforts to build trust *will* be undermined. Trust and driving people cannot coexist. If trust is the end you desire, then driving change must be the means.

WHAT'S LEFT AFTER THE CHANGE?

After driving people, whether the change is a success or a failure, we are left with change scars from the lashes of the whip. We are left with dispirited people who have learned it is easier to do as they are told so the pain will cease. We are left with people who fear the next change in management or the next election, because it will bring the next order, the next threat, the next change.

When you drive people, they shrink. They hide. It dulls their ability to choose, think, or act. They cower. They wait.

In brilliant contrast, after driving change, you and the people who collaborate with you are stronger and more unified. You've fought a battle together and won. You've climbed a mountain of change, looked from the top, and enjoyed the view—together. You learned many things about yourself and your fellow change agents along the way. You've all increased your networks, expanded your capabilities, and stretched the boundaries of what you thought was possible.

Over the years I've taught thousands about driving change, and I've had the honor of following some of them through their initial attempts at creating their changes. Each and every time, whether they ultimately succeeded or failed, those who drive change are stronger, more capable and more joyful after each attempt.

When you drive change, you grow, the people involved grow, and the change grows. The change is filled with cheerful effort and many successes.

DRIVING CHANGE IS THE ENABLER

If you are part of an organization that is seeking employee development or greater citizen participation, driving change is the enabler of the outcomes you desire.

In every comparison, driving change beats driving people.

Driving change is more effective than driving people. Hence, the first Change Agent Essential is: **Drive Change, Not People.**

Chapter 4

● ● ●

THE CHANGE PATHS

*"If you know something can't succeed, how much time and
energy are you willing to give it? Nobody goes looking
for a lost cause. You invest yourself in what you believe
can succeed. When you embrace possibility thinking, you
believe in what you're doing, and that gives you energy."*

— JOHN C. MAXWELL

Each change follows its own path, yet when we compare the paths of changes attempted by driving people with the paths of driving change, we find two distinct patterns. Allow me to show you these patterns by telling you a story about two similar but different hikes.

Both hikes are up the same mountain. Both hikes involve you. That is where the similarities end. One is based on driving people, the other on driving change.

A HIKE WHILE DRIVING PEOPLE

You've been ordered to take the hike by a senior official. The official has told you when you shall hike, how you shall hike, who must go with you, and what gear you may use. If this were the typical change in organizations today, you would be expected to hike with the corporate-approved pack filled with over 150 pounds of stuff bought at a deep discount. I like to call it the "one-size-fits-few" model. Oh, and due to budget cuts, the gear doesn't include hiking boots.

The weather report suggests rain turning to snow, but the order is the order and you must hike today.

How does the hike go?

You and your hiking companions set out from the trailhead only when you are forced to depart, and you only go far enough to be able to tell your superiors that you tried.

At the first downed tree, you don't fight your way over it. You either sit down and wait for your seniors to fix it or you turn around and head home. You followed orders; you hiked. Time to go back to work.

A HIKE WHILE DRIVING CHANGE

Let's try that hike again. This time let's try driving change.

This hike is one you'd love to go on. Your boss isn't sure this is the best path, but she won't stop you if you try it on your own. You've picked out your gear, negotiated when you'll go, and recruited others to go with you. You don't have the best gear money can buy, but you have the best the current budget could provide. You'd rather start now than wait for perfect gear or perfect conditions.

The weather report suggests rain turning to snow, but you've been looking forward to this hike and you're willing to trudge through any conditions.

How does the hike go?

You and your excited, volunteer hiking companions set out from the trailhead, enjoying yourselves even as the rain turns to snow. At the first downed tree, you and your companions come together to figure out your way around the obstacle. Once past it, you keep going. You don't rest until you're at the top of the mountain admiring the view. You look toward the next, higher mountain with awe and excitement. Another beautiful peak to climb. Off you go.

COMPARING THE CHANGE PATHS

These two hiking stories illustrate the vast difference in energy created by driving change as opposed to driving people. It was the contrast displayed in these kinds of stories that pushed me to first draw the change paths years ago.

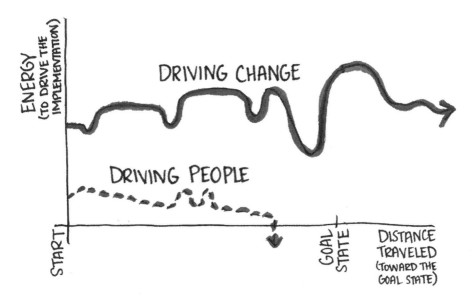

THE DRIVING PEOPLE PATH

For more than a month I had watched a good friend attempt to implement a change she believed in, but had been forced into by her boss. She had assembled, as was the status quo, a team of conscripts representing various parts of the organization.

The only reason the change wasn't at zero energy when it entered the organization was because she was still willing to try. She recruited a few others who believed in the change as she did, but they couldn't keep the momentum going when most of the team members were conscripts. The weight of the status quo of driving people was too great.

The team couldn't agree on what they should make others do first. Should they force people to take Class A, or should they experiment with Process B? Which would produce the best result? Around and around their conversations went, until finally the organization got distracted by the next big crisis and the whole change failed. After a few sad reports of faux-progress, the change was gone.

After drawing this curve and showing it to people across organizations, I found it to be universal. When changes are introduced and moved forward through driving people, the energy in the change is low and the change rarely, if ever, reaches the goal. This is the "flavor of the month" cycle that repeats, seemingly unendingly, in organizations and communities.

A policy is proposed, a committee formed, and meetings held. Steam bleeds out, the change dies, the citizens lose hope. The cycle repeats. We hope that this next time it will be different, but unfortunately, it is not.

TACTIC: ELIMINATE MANDATORY MEETINGS

You can switch paths, from driving people to driving change. Here's how.

First, you must stop driving people. One, very obvious way to do that is to cancel immediately all of the change's mandatory meetings. Yes. I said cancel them. (When I make this suggestion to people in my classes or audiences, they often gasp with fear. You may have gasped just a moment ago when you read my suggestion. That's okay. I understand your shock.)

"Then what?" you ask. "How will I accomplish my change without meetings?"

I'm not suggesting you have no meetings. I'm not opposed to meetings. I'm opposed to *mandatory* meetings.

After you cancel the mandatory meetings, I encourage you to send a meeting notice back out to all the participants, but deliberately mark each attendee as optional. Then, in the message portion of the invitation tell the attendees two things: why you care about the change and why you value their participation. Then, wait for the first optional meeting and see who attends.

See who attends?!?!

Did you just scream that out loud or only in your head?

Are you worried you'll be the only person at the meeting? That's a valid worry. Yet, I encourage you not to worry, and here's why.

If you end up alone in that meeting, you will have learned something valuable and something you probably weren't aware of during your last mandatory meeting. You were all alone then too, even though you were surrounded by people.

Now, most times when I've had a change agent act on my suggestion, they don't sit alone in their next meeting. But often, they come close.

If they had 20 people in the last mandatory meeting, this time they usually have only two people. This is actually a victory for all three, and it can be for you. How? Once you are a team of three instead of a team of 20, you are now nimble and agile enough to scramble out of the whirlpool.

Those 18 other people were supplying the energy that kept the vortex swirling. I've learned that when people are forced to attend meetings about changes they don't care about, they employ a wealth of tactics to derail progress.

I've seen people break into an agenda early in a meeting saying, "This will only take a moment, but…"—and then filibuster the rest of the meeting, entertaining themselves but accomplishing nothing. I've seen people attend meetings, open their laptops, and type away at other work rather than engage in the content at all. Meanwhile, people who felt passionate about the change were forced to sit along the wall or at the far end of the room, struggling to be heard.

A room filled with conscripted attendees hurts dialogue and discussion, and kills action. Getting consensus on action from the laptop-focused attendee or the blustering bored person is impossible. They might not admit it, but it's likely their goal for attending your meetings is only to be able to say they attended. They aren't trying to achieve anything. They may even be trying to prevent you from moving forward; and they are succeeding.

That's the double benefit of getting these conscripted, "voluntold" participants out of the room. First, you are now free of their distractions and their deadweight in your meeting. Second, you are now on your way to winning their friendship because you have given them back their time. *Now* you can concentrate on the people who truly want to be there. You can jump up to the driving change path.

THE DRIVING CHANGE PATH

Can you feel your energy rising? I've watched people switch to driving change and rise immediately in hope, energy, and enthusiasm as they cast off the weight of driving people.

When you've jumped up to the driving change line, you believe in your change and you're ready to go. You ask for others to join you.

You and your few fellow change agents are ready to set out on your change path. The path won't be smooth, but compared to the driving people path, you are working with an order of magnitude more energy. That brimming energy will carry you over the bumps you are sure to encounter along the way.

The first bumps may come when you face difficulty getting others involved or hit obstacles to implementation. Your energy and passion for your change will propel you forward. And then, it will happen.

You'll hit a big obstacle, a big dip in energy, and you'll think you can't go on.

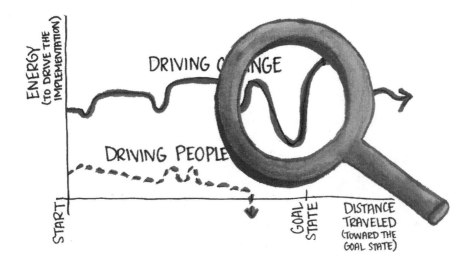

The part of the driving change path with the big dip was drawn years ago in response to a colleague showing up in my office distraught over the state of her change. She and her team had worked for over a year to build a team, craft a vision, test the change (both technically and organizationally), and prepare for full implementation.

Right before the project was set to launch, it was shut down by a senior manager who had not been briefed on the change. In the aftermath of this sudden shutdown, my colleague was feeling the lowest energy she had ever felt on this change. She didn't think she and her team could go on.

I drew the path to show her that even though she was at her lowest point, she still had energy she could tap into. She could rally, recover, and implement her change. In the end, she did. She gathered her remaining strength and met with the senior manager who opposed the change. She won the manager to the change, and the implementation proceeded.

She wasn't the first one to hit the dip in energy when driving change.

A HISTORICAL PERSPECTIVE

This is not a new pattern. We can map historical changes onto this same curve. One of my favorites is an event that occurred on August 12, 1805, on the frontier of the new American territory bought as part of the Louisiana Purchase.

Captain Meriwether Lewis and a small party from the Corps of Discovery had left Captain William Clark and the main party to travel west overland attempting to find the headwaters of the Missouri River. They had been told to expect that when they found the headwaters they would crest the ridge, hear the sea birds calling, smell the salt air, and see the ocean in view.

When Lewis climbed to the top of the ridge, however, his eyes were not met with an expanse of sea. Instead, he saw row upon row of saw-tooth mountains, on what we now know as the Idaho-Montana border. Lewis knew at that moment that the story he had put his faith in was wrong. The Pacific Ocean was much farther west than the headwaters of the Missouri River. And Lewis and his men had a much longer way to travel than anyone had predicted.

Lewis and his party were nearly starving. They needed strong horses to get them and their supplies over the mountains and to their seaside destination. They had hoped to find the Shoshone Indians earlier than this. There were signs that the Indians were close, but they had yet to see their faces. What was our daring Captain Lewis to do?

His team had traveled thousands of miles across uncharted territory on the promise that the Missouri River would lead to the Pacific Ocean. That promise was unfulfilled. To turn around was perilous, but to go on was near suicide. Winter arrives quickly in the Rocky Mountains, and some mornings the party had awoken to light dustings of snow and frost.

Did they turn around? No.

They kept going. Soon after cresting the Continental Divide, Captain Lewis and his small party finally found the Shoshone. Their chief, Cameahwait, was willing to help them, especially after he realized that the young Indian woman, Sacagawea, who had accompanied the Corps of Discovery from Fort Mandan in North Dakota, was his sister.

The Corps of Discovery got the horses they needed, along with a guide. They barely made it through the mountain pass to the western leading rivers, rafted along the difficult rapids, and floated finally to the what is now the Oregon and Washington coast. They had found and followed the mighty Columbia to where she met the sea. They got to their goal, and Captain Clark wrote in his journal, "Ocian in view! O! the joy."

I share this story with you because it puts the challenges of our changes into perspective. Yes, you might be at your lowest energy point, but you aren't on the edge of the known world facing what seems like slow death in one direction and a faster death in the other.

Most often we are facing a disgruntled coworker or an agitated fellow citizen who has just heard of our project and raises late concerns that we must address. These are obstacles, but they are not a mountain range followed by rapids leading into an unknown territory with peril on all sides.

And, we are not on the driving people path, where every obstacle is a worthy excuse to give up and go home because our energy is gone. We are, like the Corps of Discovery, volunteers who have fought for the chance to drive change. We may be at low energy, but we still have some reserves within us to keep going. And together, we have enough energy to conquer anything.

From that moment until they returned to St. Louis on September 23, 1806, every member of the Corps of Discovery survived. Though they nearly starved on their trip west through the mountains. Though the Indian tribes along the western rivers lined the shores to watch these strange men drown amongst the rapids. Though they faced a cold, wet winter on the Oregon coast, followed by the trek thousands of miles by water and land back to St. Louis. Despite all these formidable obstacles, the Lewis and Clark expedition kept going. Their story shows us what can be done through fearless commitment to a change.

Looking back, from our vantage point more than 200 years later, I continue to be amazed at their tenacity. They all volunteered for the work, and they never gave up. Their journey certainly followed the driving change path. They were only gone from St. Louis for two years and four months. Given how long it takes to get any government or organizational project complete today, we should all be amazed.

That is the power in driving change—joyful effort and a host of extraordinary successes.

DRIVING CHANGE IS NOT ENOUGH

Now that we've named the status quo (driving people), uncovered a powerful alternative (driving change), compared the two in depth, and plotted the change paths; we must confront the reality that driving change is not enough.

Chapter 5

● ● ●

THE CHANGE BUFFERS

*"I never leave things to chance. I always try to
make sure that the deck is stacked in my favor.
I put safety nets on top of safety nets."*

— *ELIYAHU M. GOLDRATT*

Project managers often protect their project success by accepting some
flexibility in one of three (sometimes four) constraints: cost, scope,
schedule, or quality. I first encountered these concepts when I studied and
implemented the Theory of Constraints, a management methodology, introduced in Eliyahu Goldratt's 1984 book, *The Goal*. In that methodology,
the applied flexibility is called a buffer.

I've found that change projects need additional layers of flexibility—
flexibility to depart from the current rules and accepted behaviors. I call
these added layers of flexibility the change buffers.

CHANGE BUFFERS

Change Buffers are explicit thoughts, behaviors, or policies that allow the change agents—as well as the change itself—to vary from the people and environment that represent the status quo.

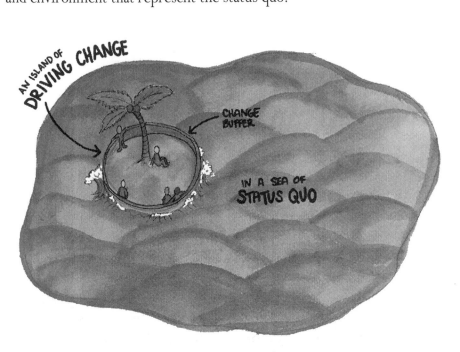

Change buffers comprise four categories:

- Personal Buffers
- Leadership Buffers
- Policy Buffers
- Celebration Buffers

It is your responsibility to build them quickly and maintain them diligently.

PERSONAL BUFFERS

A **Personal Buffer** is a buffer you can create and maintain independent of the organization related to your change. I've found and used two types of personal buffers.

When you can say, "I don't care what other people think," you've created a mindset buffer. A **Mindset Buffer** is a personal commitment to act on your change regardless of the reaction of the people or environment around it.

Saying "I don't care what other people think," is easier than believing it, and believing it seems to be easier than consistently acting on it. We all choose, at least on occasion, to be liked rather than to be effective. The few change agents, who always chose to be effective achieved and sustained true, lasting shifts in the status quo; they are the historical figures we remember. We know their names because they managed to change the world.

Admiral H. G. Rickover, founder of the U.S. Nuclear Navy, was well known for not caring what other people, including his Navy superiors, thought of him. I argue that it was a secret to his success as a change agent, because he lived firmly within his own mindset buffer and no one could deter him from his goals.

Many more of us create the second type of personal buffer, the friendship buffer. A **Friendship Buffer** is the person or persons you turn to on challenging days to strengthen your will and give you comfort and resolve to continue your change journey.

When you are driving change, you are leading from the front; and leaders get noticed. Not all of this notoriety will be positive. On the rough days, when others are sharing their negative opinions of you and you want to give up, you'll need that trusted friend. You'll need someone to call, a smiling face to visit, a reminder of why you are driving change, and a dose of encouragement to keep going. Or, you'll need a firm mindset buffer, or both.

LEADERSHIP BUFFERS

The **Leadership Buffer** is the protective wing that a leader stretches out to shelter the people who work with them. This leadership buffer is created when a leader says, "When people ask you who told you that you could be different, you tell them I did." Or who says, "In my group, we live by these values and behave this way." That sheltering leadership allows anyone who is part of the team to fall into a new line, or cluster in a new grouping—even if that grouping is vastly different from how the rest of the organization operates.

Chances are good you've worked with one of these great leaders from time to time. They're the ones you remember for how much you accomplished together. They're the ones who made everything feel different. They're the ones you thought were one in a million. They might have been, but they don't have to be.

Anyone can create a leadership buffer for someone else. You can create a leadership buffer simply by saying, "If they ask you who told you that you could do that, tell them it was me."

You create a leadership buffer whenever you offer someone access to your network of contacts. When you say, "Feel free to call Person X and tell them I gave you their name. Send them my best wishes—I know they'll help you out."

The leadership buffer is a way of implementing Step 5 of John Kotter's eight-step process, "Empower Employees for Broad-Based Action." Anyone can empower others. All you have to do is act to create space and provide protection for others to drive change.

POLICY BUFFERS

In my experience, personal and leadership buffers are what most people have relied on (whether they realized it or not) when they have created changes. Change agents attempt to power their buffers on willpower, theirs or their leader's, until the willpower runs out. Quickly, the buffer collapses. Many change agents have been caught in this situation in the past, so you can likely picture a time when it happened to you too.

Thankfully, there is a more robust, resilient buffer that change agents can build to protect their changes. A **Policy Buffer** is a deliberate policy change that permits you and your change to differ from the status quo. It is a more powerful buffer for your change than willpower, because once a policy is changed it most often stays changed.

A policy is a written or unwritten rule that people are compelled to follow. Though policies are less visible than the people involved in the change, policies are orders of magnitude more powerful than individuals in preventing or enabling a change. Why? Because policies create safe spaces for change—and these safe spaces exist regardless of who is present.

In global organizations, policy buffers are especially powerful because the policy change affects all members everywhere all at once.

An example of a policy buffer is authorizing Project X to ignore a change to Policy B until after a project milestone. Another is creating a rule where members of Group A will always complete Process Z even though members of Groups B, C, and D refuse to implement Process Z.

Years ago, I joined the union that represented the engineers at my employer, the International Federation of Professional and Technical Engineers, Local 12. As a union representative, I could ask questions of leadership that would have been inappropriate in my role as a working-level employee. Accepting the union representative title was my policy buffer. The policies surrounding what it meant to be a union representative protected my ability to act outside of my normal role.

With these examples, both specific and generic, I hope you can see that the range of possibilities for policy buffers is immense. I would contend that the policy buffer is second only to driving change as the most powerful and most underused concept in change leadership today.

CELEBRATION BUFFERS

Step 6 of Kotter's eight steps is "Generating Short-Term Wins." I define a win as any bit of progress toward your change goal. Generating those wins is great. Celebrating them is better. Few organizations celebrate—and if they do, they tend to restrict celebrations to infrequent, large events. I've found these celebrations are not enough to support change. A successful strategy is to create a celebration buffer for your change. A **Celebration Buffer** is a commitment to frequently notice, define, and celebrate wins related to your change.

Kotter, via Step 6, challenges us to take notice of the progress we make along the way toward our goal—and to call attention to it. Kotter found, and I have validated, that people amidst a change need this sense of progress to sustain their energy.

The people involved in a change often report to the same desk or home from the first day of the journey to the last day. How will they know they are making progress if you don't call attention to it and help them to do the same? Help them celebrate the progress, and they will move faster and with greater energy.

PLAYGROUND CELEBRATIONS

In early 2011, when we founded Bremerton Beyond Accessible Play, we didn't know how long the project would take. We did know that celebrations of our progress would move us forward faster. So, over the three and a half years of the project, we celebrated every project anniversary with a big party. These large celebrations complemented smaller celebrations we held when we hit milestones, made new partnerships, or chose playground equipment. Through the celebrations, we gave ourselves and our project partners more confidence, energy, and joy. In our meetings one of us would often shout, "Win!" after someone reported progress. We kept ourselves energized and moving forward. You can too.

TACTIC: CLAIM YOUR WINS EACH WEEK

A simple way to implement a celebration buffer for your change is to dedicate time each week to sharing with your change team what each person considers their wins. The celebrations add fuel to the tanks of your fellow change agents; they help your team to continue moving forward.

You, as the change agent, need to measure and value the worth of your change work. Celebrate your wins; don't wait for others to do it for you. Expecting others to decide whether your work has value leaves you vulnerable to the fickle interests of others not invested in your change. (If they were, wouldn't they have joined your change team by now?) Don't give them that much power over you.

Celebrate your wins. Celebrate your team's wins. The wins can be small ("We got four new members this week.") or big ("We just won several million dollars in new funding!"). The important part isn't the size of the win, or who else will notice. What's important is that *you* notice—and that you help your team to notice, too.

READY FOR ACTION

As you plan your change, remember to invest time in building your change buffers. Often, you'll need more than one.

I've watched many change agents, energetic about driving their change, rush forward rashly without change buffers and without a plan. When they act before they plan, they run headlong into sharp obstacles that rob them of their power and joy, not to mention the success of their change.

You can do better.

Creating and maintaining these change buffers is an essential step to protect the fledgling change until the status quo shifts to support it. Hence, the second Change Agent Essential is: **Create and Maintain Change Buffers**.

Part 2

PLANNING

*"More than ambition, more than ability, it is rules that limit
contribution; rules are the lowest common denominator of
human behavior. They are a substitute for rational thought."*

— ADMIRAL H.G. RICKOVER

Planning for change when you're driving people is all about determining what other people should do or stop doing, usually without their involvement and in excruciating detail. If this method was ever effective, it was certainly in personal, organizational, community, national, or world systems that were less connected and slower-changing. That world is gone.

The long list of orders that others must follow, a common outcome of driving people, reminds me of traffic lights telling drivers when to go and stop, purportedly to keep the drivers safe and the traffic flowing, while actually choking flow and giving an artificial sense of safety.

There's an urban art installation in London, England, by French artist Pierre Vivant featuring 75 traffic lights mounted on a single central pole, each giving a conflicting signal of stop, caution, GO! It's a great metaphor for what actually happens when one or more changes implemented by driving people are happening to us at the same time.

I think copies of Vivant's work should be installed in scattered locations around the world to remind us all of the fallacy of driving people in an interconnected world. We cannot create flow, motion, or accomplishment with disconnected multitudes of orders. That era is gone. It's time for something new.

In early spring, 2016, my work took me to Swindon, England, home of the Magic Roundabout, a transportation marvel. It is a roundabout of roundabouts, a central traffic circle surrounded by five smaller ones. Its custom design, tailored to the location and topography, is a solution to address modern traffic demands of an infrastructure built during a slower time. It is a great metaphor for the challenges we face today when we are trying to create flow amidst artifacts of the past.

Today, Swindon's Magic Roundabout neatly handles the community's entire traffic flow. At different times of day, the system of traffic circles allows drivers to adapt to the real-time conditions around them. By leveraging flexibility within its boundaries, the drivers traveling through the Magic Roundabout can achieve flow even in extreme high-traffic conditions.

Sally, a friend from Swindon, told me that she is a "Magic Roundabout expert" because she has driven through it so often. She can spot the new drivers. They take a slower, but eventually effective, route through. Meanwhile, using her expert skills, Sally quickly surveys the traffic pattern and darts through. She follows the same rules as the new drivers, but optimizes her speed by leveraging her practiced skill.

While others in your life are sitting at the intersection of change watching the tower of lights waiting, waiting, waiting for their light to turn green; you can become like Sally, an expert at creating flow.

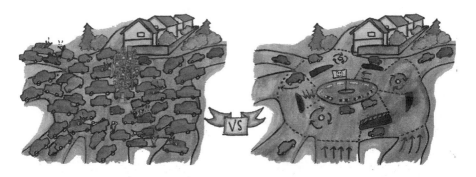

You may be thinking, "But someone had to *create* the Magic Roundabout for Sally. I'm surrounded by traffic lights. How can I begin to create change flow?"

To begin to achieve this kind of optimal flow, you don't have to remake the world around you. You need only to look at your world with fresh eyes.

In October, 2012, Hurricane Sandy hit the east coast of the United States, causing large areas to lose power. All the traffic lights went dark. I was following the news coverage of the storm aftermath when I saw a story that caught my eye.

In Nassau County, New York, someone or some group (likely the public works employees), had constructed a roundabout out of orange cones in a large intersection where lights stood dark without power. I'm sure this was only a temporary change until the power could be restored to the lights, but it serves as a bright example of a real-world implementation of my claim that you can go without the lights and try a new way to improve the flow.

We must create movement, flow, and results amongst artifacts of our past; but we don't have to demolish the past to make way for the future. We can, instead, reimagine how we might achieve flow, just like those resourceful workers who designed the roundabout amongst the darkened lights.

We will plan the change, get moving, dissolve excuses, create concrete goals, check for settlers, and draw boundaries. We will do all of this without having to dismantle any of the current status quo methods. We can leave those to the others. We now have a better way.

Chapter 6

• • •

ACT TODAY AND DISSOLVE EXCUSES

"Do what you can, with what you've got, where you are."

— WILLIAM *"SQUIRE BILL"* WIDENER

n his 1913 autobiography, Theodore Roosevelt, the 26th President of the United States, quoted "a bit of homely philosophy" from one of his contemporaries, William "Squire Bill" Widener: "Do what you can, with what you've got, where you are." Widener's advice, offered by Roosevelt as practical wisdom for living a purposeful, happy life, makes for a perfect change agent motto.

If we personalize it, it reads:

I will do what I can, with what I have, where I am.

That's my change agent motto.

It's easy to say, and it's enough. It reminds me—and it can remind you—that we have all the power, potential, and possibilities we need to begin our change today. We do. You do.

You can do what you can, with what you have, where you are, to create your change. Believe it and you can change your world.

THE PLAYGROUND PROJECT BEGINS

When we started the playground project, we didn't have much: not much time, not much money, and not much understanding of what a playground project would require. What we did have was a willingness to try to make the change—along with the foundational concept of driving change and the reminder to do what we could, with what we had, where we were.

Here's what I remember. I think it was a Thursday. I know it was February, 2011. My friend, Stephanie Johnson, called me after taking her son, Matthew, to the closest accessible playground, 40 minutes away from Bremerton.

Stephanie told me how much fun Matthew had playing on the accessible equipment. He didn't even have to leave his wheelchair! His sisters had been able to play with him, finally. This was the first time they had all played together at a playground. At typical playgrounds, Matthew could only sit in his wheelchair and watch his sisters play.

Stephanie said, "April, let's build a playground." I answered, "Okay," and thus our three-and-a-half-year journey began.

In the next few days Stephanie and I tried to figure out what we could do, with what we had, where we were. We acted. First we called a few of our close friends who also have children with special needs. We asked if they wanted to join us. They did. Our change was moving. Win!

Next, we had to dissolve the excuses that might have slowed or stopped us.

DISSOLVE EXCUSES

When I meet change agents in organizations and communities around the world, I find people with ideas that are ready for the world—but they as change agents are stuck. They seem tied in place with ropes of excuses.

Their varied excuses typically include:
- An authority figure (e.g., manager, elected official) won't allow the change.
- I'm not powerful enough to create the change.
- There's no budget for the change.
- The rules prevent the change.
- The culture doesn't support the change.
- There's no time for the change.
- Others won't let the change happen.

In this chapter, we'll challenge each of these excuses one by one and dissolve them.

Russell Ackoff, organizational theorist and author of *The Art of Problem Solving*, differentiated solving (fighting to win) or resolving (compromising to a fair agreement) from dissolving (changing the conditions that produced the excuse so that it disappears). Dissolving is a higher-leverage action than solving or resolving, so we'll focus on that tactic.

AN AUTHORITY FIGURE WON'T ALLOW THE CHANGE

"Authority Figure X wouldn't let that happen, or wouldn't let me do it." The change agents who have given me this excuse usually declared it with immense confidence.

I would reply with a simple question: "Did you ask Authority Figure X?" Overwhelmingly, their answer was "No."

I think it is terribly unfair to blame an authority figure for stopping your change when you haven't even asked them about it. The way to dissolve this excuse is simply to ask Authority Figure X, "Will you support my change?"

Now, should Authority Figure X say no, your next question can be, "Why?" or the more effective, "What would have to change about Change C or the environment around Change C for you to support it?"

That's a "Yes, if…" question instead of a "No, because…" question. "Yes, if…" questions are better because they get Authority Figure X thinking more deeply about your change. "Yes, if…" questions require those in authority to imagine an idea working, rather than to dismiss it without further thought.

Once you've asked Authority Figure X directly if they can support your change—and have gotten their answer to "Yes, if…"—you're now in a position to shift your change from stopped to started. Your task then is to meet the conditions Authority Figure X set.

Now, many change agents get frustrated when they are given any conditions to earn their authority figure's support. They want unconditional support or none at all. I encourage you not to take this all-or-nothing course. Most often, when you pursue all or nothing, you get nothing. Leave those all-or-nothing fights to the people who are driving people. You're better than that. You're driving change.

I'M NOT POWERFUL ENOUGH TO CREATE THE CHANGE

Once they have the support of any authority figure, change agents often become afraid of leading their own change. I've heard people from the bottom to the top argue that they are powerless to create the change they seek. New hires will lament that they lack seniority. Executives will lament that they aren't the Chief Executive Officer. CEOs will lament that they aren't the Chairman of the Board.

At bottom, this excuse is an attempt to give yourself permission to stop before you have to dare mightily to create your change. It's an excuse that says, "Until the world grants me the authority, I can't succeed." Quit waiting for the world! You can succeed; expect it.

Who are you not to try? Whether you are a mother, a father, a citizen, a mayor, a club president, a local member, a tradesperson, or a union leader; you can do wonderful and powerful things if only you'll try.

This is an easy excuse to overcome, because you need only to convince one person to stop believing it: you. Will you do it? Will you believe you can succeed at creating your change?

Sure, maybe if you had those authority positions, you'd have access to more budget, more publicity, more networks. But you'd also have more expectations, more competing issues, and more of something else you can't even see. The truth is, there is no "right" position from which to drive a change; there is only an individual who *believes* they are the right person—and who acts on that belief. *That's* the power. You possess that power.

At the start of the playground project, we were plagued with self-doubt. Many of us thought, "Who are we to build a playground, while working full-time, mothering our kids, coordinating their complicated care, and more?"

We pushed forward with our change despite our worries and doubts. Nowadays, those uncertain parents who first led Bremerton Beyond Accessible Play don't worry or doubt themselves or their capabilities as change agents.

THERE'S NO BUDGET FOR THE CHANGE

All changes start without a budget. Remember that when you encounter this excuse. When people tell me, "There's no budget," I always agree. "Yes. You're right." Then I add, "So what?"

They look at me stunned. Their argument is that nothing happens without a budget. They're partially right.

Often, to complete the change, you will need some budget to cover purchases, events, and sustainment costs. Yet, you don't need that funding simply to start. Every change begins with a budget of zero. Every one.

The step from zero budget to some budget is the first challenge. How big should the step be? From zero to one million? Recalling the encouragement to do what we can, with what we have, where we are, I encourage you to start with the size of the step that you can quickly and comfortably take toward the budget you need.

With the playground project, we started with a $300 step. We went from having no money to having $300, a donation from a local management organization, the Naval Civilian Managers Association. I had recently held elected office in the local chapter. Therefore, I knew what sorts of causes they supported and how to approach them for a donation. Less than a month after starting the playground project, we had our first donation. This is not the way most people start their projects.

I've found most change agents start their projects by defining how much total budget they think they'll need to complete the project. For the sake of carrying our example through, let's say it is $500,000, roughly the final budget for the playground project. Using this $500,000 value, a typical change team will spend months creating an elaborate plan to obtain it in the largest chunks possible. Huge grant applications would be written. Big donors would be courted. Much planning, much discussing, and some action would happen. In the meantime, their budget sits at zero and their progress is nearly zero, too.

What we did instead—and what I encourage you to do instead—is to get some budget, as small a budget as you can raise quickly—and get the change moving. We turned that $300 first donation into over $500,000 in three and a half years. It's not where you start, but where you end, that matters.

The other challenge to the lack of budget excuse is to re-examine from which source you are gaining and spending money. I've talked to change agents who wanted to attend a training class but lacked room within their quarterly training budget. When they brought the excuse to me we started to dissolve it by expanding the constraints they put around the idea of the budget.

First I asked, "Can you be flexible with the quarterly budget if you stay within your yearly budget?"

Then we expanded the budget scope by asking, "Can you be flexible with the training budget if you protect the project budget?"

Third we challenged, "Can you be flexible on the project budget if you protect the delivery date, and therefore revenue?"

Finally we implored, "Can we create the change if we find a budget from another source outside your budget area?"

This kind of re-examination doesn't always result in funding for what you're hoping to accomplish, but it does show you where the flexibilities and the funding constraints lie in your organization. That learning will allow you to fund future changes faster and more robustly than you would have done without attempting to make your first change. In that case, the budget excuse isn't entirely dissolved, but it *is* reduced—and next time it can be dissolved entirely.

THE RULES PREVENT THE CHANGE

Another common challenge to our changes is the belief that some rule prohibits the change. I say "belief" because when pressed for which rule it is, and where is it written down, most people cannot find a documented rule that prohibits the change.

TACTIC: SEARCH FOR THE RULE

When I've asked people to show me the rule, I often hear, "Well, I don't know where it is, but I know it exists." When you hear this kind of statement, I challenge you to do a rule search. Set a fixed amount of time, perhaps a few days, for the search—and list some likely places where you might find either the pertinent rules or some experts on the rules. With those parameters set, you can begin your search.

If, after exhausting the time period, you haven't found a rule, written or implied, I challenge you to decide whether you will act on the change or not. If you choose to act, then you can be strong in the knowledge that if you do discover a prohibitive rule later, you will at least have done appropriate due diligence. That is often protection enough from the worry of violating a rule. If you choose at that point not to act, then you may be stopping for a ghost. It's your choice.

A funny, sad fact is that in most cases no written rule exists at all to prohibit your change. And rarely is there ever a law, ordinance, or regulation that blocks a change. Most often, when the change agents I've worked with have found something we can loosely call a rule, it is an unwritten rule. These "ways we've always done it" only *appear* to be steel; they are usually mere mush.

How can I say this? Because, if a "way we've always done it" is worth continuing as "the way we do it," it should be strong enough to withstand inspection. If it cannot, it deserves to be overturned. Many times I've found these legacies of the past hurting individuals, organizations and communities. They keep us from achieving the outcomes we want now. Most of these unwritten rules have outlived their usefulness and need to be purged. Without courageous change agents willing to dissolve excuses, they will never be.

DISSOLVING RULES TO BUILD THE PLAYGROUND

During the playground project we ran into two unwritten rules that were challenged and overturned for the benefit of the children and adults with special needs in Kitsap County.

The first was an unwritten, but widely held, rule that each community club (for example, the Rotarians, the Kiwanis, the Lions) would provide support for playgrounds only to the park that was named for them. Hence, the Rotary was expected to fund improvements at Evergreen Rotary Park, the Lions at Lions Park, and so on. When we first brought the playground project to these community clubs, the status quo answer was, "We support projects only at our park." This rule had served the clubs well over the years to keep their members focused and their donors clear on where their funds would be used.

We complimented the club members for their devotion to the community and suggested that in our case, the needs of the children for one playground now should outweigh the rule that kept their focus separate. We said, "This playground is where *all* may play and where the community can come together."

We asked the club leaders to see their boundaries not at the edges of their parks but at the edges of the city—and to join together to speed the project along. They all responded, broke with tradition, and contributed to our project, which happened to be located at Evergreen Rotary Park.

The second rule also came from a local community group, the Kiwanis Club of Bremerton, and their partner group, the Bennett Memorial Scholarship Fund. It was their operating rule to accept applications from students wishing to attend college and to provide some scholarships only to those applicants.

In late 2013, Bremerton Beyond Accessible Play had some tough choices to make. We had enough funding to begin to build our playground in the summer of 2014, but we were $30,000 short of fully funding the list of playground equipment we desired.

At our usual monthly meeting, we were diligently sorting the equipment into Phase 1 and Phase 2 purchases. Rebekah Uhtoff, our Vice President and Design Chair, showed obvious emotion as she recommended we include in Phase 2 her son Gabe's most hoped-for piece of equipment, a roller table, which would allow Gabe to scoot around freely on his back. Sunny Wheeler, a member of Bremerton Beyond Accessible Play, the Kiwanis Club, and the Bennett Memorial Scholarship Fund's board, remembers being moved to tears.

Sunny recalls, "The talk of sacrifice and the thought that the playground would not be fully inclusive motivated me to make my pitch to the Bennett Memorial Scholarship Fund to ask them to invest in the futures and education of children that may never have the opportunity to attend college....Play is the first and most important way all children learn."

She asked them to break with their rule and provide $10,000 in funding for the playground. They voted to fund much more.

On a cold, rainy December night, Rebekah and I stood in the front of the Bremerton City Council chamber presenting the Phase 1 funding. As we turned to return to our seats, a councilman said, "Wait! I think there are some people here to present something too." Sunny and her fellow Bennett Memorial Scholarship Fund board members rose, came forward, and surprised us all with the full $30,000 we needed for Phase 2.

I'll freely admit that I was overcome by emotion and wept (and it wasn't just because I was four months pregnant at the time). When the rules fall away and the outcomes emerge, it is a powerful event, full of possibility, hope, and joy. I hope you will experience one of these moments with your change. You can, if you challenge the rules and dissolve the excuses.

THE CULTURE DOESN'T SUPPORT THE CHANGE

When people say, "The culture doesn't support the change," they are offering the thinnest of excuses. It is a gambit to end the conversation, like telling someone their solution is "like trying to solve world hunger," or "like trying to boil the ocean." The statement kills the argument by implying it is impossible even to consider the solutions. The excuse is thin because a blanket statement like "The culture doesn't support the change," is typically used to extinguish the most plausible changes, not the most farfetched.

I once coached a colleague through this exact situation. He had tried to implement a new process, and one of the leaders had said, "That will take a culture change." The change agent had come to me dejected, ready to give up. I asked just one question.

"How many people would have to change their behaviors daily or weekly to adopt the process change?"

He started counting...2...6...12...25. He calculated that 25 people would have to change their weekly behavior. At this answer, I admit I began to giggle.

Our conversation continued with planning how he could quickly, personally speak to the 25 people, either one at a time or in small groups, to discuss their feelings about the change. He said it would take about a week. He then agreed to go begin the conversations. A few days later he reported how much progress he had already made.

I'm convinced that change agents, and those who regularly coach change agents, tend to make changes appear much more daunting than they really are. We will cover this point more in an upcoming chapter, but for now let's end by admitting that "culture" is often an excuse to end the conversation. Don't let it stop you. You and your change are better than that. Probe what, and more importantly who, must change—and you'll quickly find a way to dissolve the culture excuse.

THERE'S NO TIME FOR THE CHANGE

In the first chapter, we covered some of the ways that people will argue there is no time to drive change. We're covering it again because it comes up over and over. To dissolve this excuse, we need to borrow from the Greeks and their two words for time.

Chronos refers to clock time, the seven days, 168 hours, 10,080 minutes, or 604,800 seconds we each get each week. Chronos is indifferent to who we are and what we hope to accomplish.

Kairos is different. Kairos is the "right or opportune moment" we create to accomplish our goals. It's the time we make for the things that are important to us: our relationships, our career, our hobbies, or our changes. It is the time that pauses and slows as we enter those extraordinary intervals of joy. It's the time we create to plan, build, and finish the work we set out to do.

When I coach change agents, we create a schedule of their week and mark out the chronos time and how they are spending or investing it. Then we create a list of the things that are important to them—whether for their life in general or their change in particular—and we work together to make time for the important activities. You can do this same chronos vs. kairos plan too.

Steven Covey tells a story about a jar filled with rocks, pebbles, sand, and water. In the story a teacher instructs a student to fill an empty jar with an amount of water, then sand, then pebbles, and finally some rocks. Following this process the student is unable to fit the rocks into the jar.

The student is then given an identical empty jar and asked to begin again. This time, the student starts with the rocks, then pebbles, then sand, then water. It all fits.

That process is how you find time for the change you want to achieve in your life and in the lives of those around you. You don't try to shove the rock of your change in on top of everything else. You build your time around it and drop what doesn't fit and what doesn't need to fit.

TACTIC: TAKE CHARGE OF YOUR TIME

When you try this new kind of scheduling, you'll at first be shocked by how much of your time is spent on repeating the past without considering its value to today. Start by focusing on all recurring meetings on your calendar that lack an end date. These meeting series will steal your time until you or the organization dies (whichever comes first), unless you take action now. How many of these series can be stopped or modified to reflect a worthy investment of time to results delivered? My guess is many, if not most.

Take charge of your chronos and kairos and you'll dissolve your "no time" excuse. Now, you will still hit the physical limit of your week, but let it be where you *choose* to hit it versus where the default settings have pushed you.

When you expand out to dealing with other people's claims of no time to support your change, you can use this similar method with them or start with something even simpler. Ask them, "What time waste on your calendar would you like me to try to get rid of that would free up some time to work with me on this change?"

See if they can tell you what is wasting their time. If they cannot identify the time-wasters, then they aren't in charge of their calendar; their calendar is in charge of them. If they can define the time-wasters, help them to take the action necessary to eliminate them. Even if you fail to remove the offending time-waster, the other person will see that you are committed to helping them find time to support the change, rather than just piling more calendar demands on top of their existing workload.

OTHERS WON'T LET THE CHANGE HAPPEN

When all else fails, the sad, nameless scapegoats around us, "they" get the last bit of blame for our lack of action. In organizations, "they" are often the support organizations, like finance, information technology (IT), human resources (HR), facilities or corporate services. Or perhaps "they" are the biggest boogeyman of all: management (if you are an employee) or employees (if you are in management).

The declarations that "IT won't let us," or in the community "the city council will never approve," are often taken as true without proof. Make yourself and others prove these claims.

When you are passionate about your change, you can move past these vague declarations of opposition and test the facts. Does the entire IT department—the tens, hundreds, or thousands of people who comprise it—really oppose your change? I'll hold out the possibility that once in a million times everyone in IT would be standing in opposition to your change. Most of the time, I find, there are fewer than ten people who must be convinced to support your change. Often enough, no one opposes it. You merely assumed they would.

TACTIC: OPPOSITION CENSUS

The fastest way to dissolve the "They won't allow it," excuse is to define who *they* are, by number and by name. Conduct what I call an Opposition Census. The scope of how many people you need to win to your change, and the size of their opposition, if any, will shrink.

Start by guessing at who, exactly, might oppose you, and then go directly to them and ask, "Can you support Change X? Support means…."

I've used the Opposition Census many, many times. Only a few weeks ago, a change agent and I reduced his assumed opposition from thousands of engineers spread across a global organization to a potential opposition group of only 25 people that he works with on a weekly basis. When he checked with each of them directly, he found little resistance.

In every Opposition Census you'll find a mix of people who oppose you, who are indifferent, or who support you. In all cases you'll gain vital information, an asset instead of an excuse.

THE EXCUSES ARE DISSOLVED

Having dissolved the excuses, you are free to act. You have gained the freedom to do what you can, with what you have, where you are, in the fierce urgency of now. You can name, confront, and dissolve your excuses. You can set out on your change journey.

Now, which way will you go? How will people find you should they want to join in the change?

Chapter 7

● ● ●

SET YOUR CONCRETE GOAL

"It is less possible to second guess or dispute simple, direct ideas."

— JEFFREY PFEFFER AND ROBERT I. SUTTON

All improvement requires change, but not all change is improvement. Many change agents miss the imbalance.

I find that many changes, built on the status quo of driving people, started out as "problem-fixing" but quickly morphed into "people-fixing." The change goal, if written down, would read:

Change C's goal is to fix Process X by fixing Person A.

By contrast, a change goal built on driving change keeps the emphasis on the change, the result, and the people who will benefit.

CONCRETE GOAL

When these change attributes are summarized in one statement, I call it a **Concrete Goal**.

A concrete goal follows closely to this pattern:

BY (DATE),
(WHO) WILL... (SEE,
TOUCH, HEAR, TASTE,
EXPERIENCE OR KNOW)
(WHAT) (WHERE).

I call it a concrete goal because it is formed, cured, and made stable. It provides anyone encountering the change a clear understanding of what improvement you are working toward.

Many change agents, partway through a change, revise their concrete goal. That's okay. It's better to revise it as you learn new information and choose from amongst your various options. However, there should be only one concrete goal at a time; otherwise you'll risk creating confusion about your change.

One concrete goal exists in sharp contrast to the two common ways you might confuse people about your change. The first way is to have no goal or only a vague idea of where you are going. The second way is to have an immensely detailed plan.

Without a concrete goal (or with only a vague one), your change becomes an endless wandering journey toward an uncertain destination. I call this the Alice in Wonderland problem. In Lewis Carroll's *Alice in Wonderland*, the lost and wandering Alice encounters an enigmatic guide, the Cheshire Cat. The scene goes something like this:

Alice asks the cat, "Would you tell me, please, which way I ought to go from here?"

"That depends a good deal on where you want to get to," said the Cat.

"I don't much care where—" said Alice.

"Then it doesn't matter which way you go," said the Cat.

"—so long as I get somewhere," Alice added as an explanation.

"Oh, you're sure to do that," said the Cat, "if you only walk long enough."

On the other extreme, I've met change agents who have spent days, weeks, and months creating detailed plans for every step they'll take on a journey they haven't even started. This option is as unhelpful as (if not worse than) the Alice in Wonderland problem. At least Alice had the opportunity for adventure. In the case of the over-planned change agent, all serendipity and opportunity have been ruled out. Blech!

Let's stick to our golden mean of a concrete goal, solid enough to be useful, breakable enough to be adjusted as we learn along our journey.

It is simple to create your concrete goal. The first step is to close your eyes. (Okay, you can't read and close your eyes at the same time....This works better in the workshops. Humor me, and read these next few paragraphs. *Then* close your eyes and try this little exercise.)

After you close your eyes, imagine you have just crawled into bed after a long day working on your change. You've put in such hard work that you've earned the respect of a magician who waves a wand and grants you your change while you are sleeping. You awake in the morning, open your eyes, rise and return to where your change should be. How can you tell the change has happened?

What did you see?

What did you hear?

What did you smell, touch, taste?

What did you suddenly know or experience?

For the playground project, the core of our concrete goal was, "will experience a beyond accessible playground." We defined *beyond accessible* as a place that would be inclusive and challenging for all who experience it.

This sensory recognition of your change is the core of your concrete goal. You, and those impacted by your change, must know somehow that it has happened. With those recognizable sensations set and articulated, you can now smooth the edges of your concrete goal.

WHO AND WHERE - BE SPECIFIC

Soggy changes that rot before they ever get the chance to make an impact have soggy definitions of whom they will benefit and where they will occur. The soggy definitions of who and where create more work, more confusion, and fewer results than changes with firm definitions of *who* and *where*.

Companies often make grand claims like, "Company X shall invest Y in Program B for its employees." Its employees around the world cheer. Yet what the company really meant was that only employees in the head-quarters country would receive the investment.

Government officials declare, "Program C will benefit all citizens," when Program C is actually open only to citizens in Region Y who meet certain criteria.

Change agents say, "All of Business Group X shall adopt Method A," even though very few of the people of Business Group X need to adopt Method A to get the benefit of Method A for the entire business group.

The antidote to the sogginess, the way to embed firmness, is to start your change with the smallest group necessary and the most specific location possible. Let your words describe exactly who you have in mind and where you have in mind. Never assume people will know what you meant if you use vague language.

My directive to use the smallest group possible and the most specific location possible clashes with accepted practices in most organizations, communities, and nations, which like to reward big proclamations. The rewards go to the grandest-sounding decrees because people often don't stick around to check the results.

I'm not the first change agent to pinpoint this conflict. In 1982, Admiral H.G. Rickover called this the "Say-Do Gap". In his final testi-mony to Congress, he lamented that he was searching vainly for the man who does what he says. You can be that rare kind of change agent Admiral Rickover was seeking.

The mark of a true change agent is one who values outcomes ahead of proclamations. To gain outcomes, be specific about the *who* and the *where* in your concrete goal.

In our playground project, we specified our *who* and *where* as "children and adults with special needs" and "in Bremerton, Washington, at Evergreen Rotary Park." With these additions it read,

> By <date> children and adults with special needs will experience a beyond accessible playground in Bremerton, Washington, at Evergreen Rotary Park.

With that concrete goal we built a following, a project fund, and, ultimately, a playground. How quickly we would build it, though, would depend on the date established for our concrete goal.

BEWARE AGGRESSIVE DATES

Many change agents believe they need to set aggressive dates for their changes. It's good to challenge yourself and your change team, but beware setting aggressive dates without providing a wealth of capability and flexibility. Otherwise, you can quickly break people's spirits.

In his book *Good to Great*, Jim Collins retells the poignant prisoner of war survival story of Admiral James Stockdale and his men. Collins asked Stockdale to describe the men whose spirits broke while in captivity. Stockdale replied, "...[T]he ones who said, 'We're going to be out by Christmas.' And Christmas would come, and Christmas would go. Then they'd say, 'We're going to be out by Easter.' And Easter would come, and Easter would go. And then Thanksgiving, and then it would be Christmas again. And they died of a broken heart."

Stockdale continued, "That is a very important lesson. You must never confuse faith that you will prevail in the end—which you can never afford to lose—with the discipline to confront the brutal facts of your current reality, whatever they might be." Collins called this the Stockdale Paradox.

You've no doubt seen situations where a team's spirit has been crushed by an aggressive date unmatched by capabilities or flexibilities to achieve it. It often looks something like this:

Change Agent C doesn't control when Capability Y arrives, but wants to set an aggressive date for delivery.

Change Agent C tells Team M that they will receive Capability Y by the end of March so they can accomplish their project goal by the end of September.

March comes, and March goes.

Change Agent C now promises Capability Y in June. The project goal remains the end of September.

June comes, and June goes.

Finally, if Capability Y arrives at all, it arrives too late to save the project. Team M fails to meet the delivery date.

As change agents, we may want to set aggressive dates, but we must beware confusing the faith we will prevail with a denial of the brutal facts in front of us. Without the budget to buy needed supplies, without resources to complete key tasks in a project, and without time to allow flowers to bloom, paint to dry, or children to grow, we cannot gain the success of our change. We must confront the Stockdale Paradox, working toward our win while declaring the brutal facts and adjusting the date accordingly.

BEWARE DELAYED DATES

Faced with the threat of crushing the spirits of the people, should you set delayed dates and give people as much time as they ask for to create the change? No.

Many changes cannot be delayed because they must meet product delivery timelines or regulatory compliance dates. Nearly everyone is familiar with these reasons not to delay changes. There are other negative impacts of delayed dates, too.

STUDENT SYNDROME

When a student receives a month to complete an assignment for the teacher and starts the task not on the first day of the month, but on the night before the due date, the student has fallen ill with Student Syndrome. This syndrome attacks everyone equally—whether students, employees, managers, or elected officials. Delayed due dates feed the disease. Whenever someone thinks there is "more than enough" time, they will squander it until there is not enough. That's the negative effect of Student Syndrome: the unnecessary waste of precious time.

PARKINSON'S LAW

In 1955, a British economist and humorist C. Nothcote Parkinson coined his eponymous dictum, Parkinson's Law, which says, "Work expands so as to fill the time available for its completion." In other words, if you think you have a year to complete a change you won't insist on overcoming that obstacle this month. Instead, you'll let that side project or minor issue take up the whole monthly meeting. I've seen Parkinson's Law flourish when full-time change agents are assigned to push changes in organizations. Suddenly, a change that a small volunteer committee was working on in their free time now includes a multitude of meetings, reports, processes, and other "administrivia," which drain the organization of hours, days, and weeks of precious time.

Parkinson's Law and Student Syndrome have robbed many a change agent of the timing that would have made their change a true improvement. Don't allow yourself to be robbed. Beware delayed dates.

A situation where delayed dates squander the potential of a change often looks something like this:

It's January. Change Agent C doesn't control when Capability Y arrives, so doesn't want to over-promise on its arrival.

February arrives. Change Agent C tells Team M that they will receive Capability Y by July at the latest, just in time for them to accomplish their project goal by the end of September.

March, April, and May pass quickly without another thought to Capability Y.

In June, Team M asks for the status of receiving Capability Y by July. Change Agent C is scrambling to obtain Capability Y, but is encountering many unplanned delays.

In July, Change Agent C tells Team M that Capability Y won't be available until October.

Team M fails to meet the delivery date.

AS SOON AS POSSIBLE

If aggressive dates have danger and delayed dates have danger, what are we change agents to do? I encourage you instead to set the date of your concrete goal to be "as soon as possible."

Many of you will recognize "as soon as possible" as the full-description of the often used acronym ASAP. I do not advocate for ASAP, because it long ago lost its independent meaning and instead is translated as "NOW!" with all capitals and an exclamation point for emphasis.

By comparison, "as soon as *possible*" keeps its meaning. I truly mean that I want the outcome of my concrete goal as soon as *possible*, with heavy emphasis on a discussion of what is *possible*.

When your change requires the help of a specially talented person and you ask for the help of this person, you and they are negotiating what is possible.

I've sat through negotiations where the change agent has said,

We want to finish Change A as soon as possible.

Without the help of Person B, the soonest Change A can finish in three weeks from now.

With the help of Person B this week, Change A can finish this week.

When you define your "as soon as possible" options with clear tradeoffs, you enroll Person B, and Person B's boss, in the success of your change. They can clearly see how their support improves your results. People love to be able to claim credit for contributing to successful results. Let them. You'll both win.

THE PLAYGROUND AS SOON AS POSSIBLE

When we set our concrete goal for the playground project, we used "as soon as possible." In full, our concrete goal read:

By as soon as possible children and adults with special needs will experience a beyond accessible playground in Bremerton, Washington at Evergreen Rotary Park.

This concrete goal proved powerful for us in driving our change forward. Here are two anecdotes that demonstrate its power.

The first occurred on an average sort of day about two years into the change. I ran into a local man whom I had served with years earlier on a school district citizens committee. He asked, as many people do of capital-intensive change projects, "How is fundraising going?"

I replied, "Our goal is to build the accessible playground at Evergreen Rotary Park as soon as possible. Every dollar given today pulls that date forward to be sooner than it would be without it."

The man's response was remarkable. He reached into his pocket, took out his wallet, and gave me all the cash he had in it. He said, "This is my contribution today to help that "as soon as possible" day happen as soon as possible."

If you've struggled through a multi-year fundraising effort before, you probably gasped at this anecdote. I gasped when it happened. The local man's immediate generosity literally took my breath away.

The second story involves a conversation I heard about from Rae Ann Randall, a member of Bremerton Beyond Accessible Play.

Rae Anne served as an elected official of the Bremerton Central Lions Club. The club was debating how much to donate to the playground project and when to make the donation. They were considering two options: to wait until a later year to give a donation, or to give less the first year and more in later years. Rae Anne leveraged our "as soon as possible" concrete goal to encourage the club to a third option: authorize a donation of as much as possible as soon as possible to propel the playground project forward.

She won the argument. They chose a larger, immediate amount. The Bremerton Central Lions Club's donation made a big difference. Our playground was built sooner because of them.

Though we were often encouraged to make our goal "In five years, we will...," we refused. Instead, we stuck to, "as soon as possible," and opened our playground three and a half years after we began. I'm convinced that if we had said, "In five years…" we would still be fundraising, and the children would not be playing on the playground today.

BEYOND YOUR CONTROL

Whether aggressive, delayed, or as soon as possible, you must keep in sharp focus what is within your control and what is not. This sharp focus should be included in the concrete goal, or in the supporting information that frames it—for you, your change team, and others who may be interested in joining the change.

If a handoff date between your change and another group is set, maintain that date. Adjust your concrete goal, revising the *what*, *where*, who, or *how* to make the date possible. If any of those parameters is fixed as well, leverage the flexibility in all of the remaining flexible parameters until that flexibility is used up.

The concrete goal will help you declare what you can do, what you can't do, and what can only be done with the help of others. Now your task is to create your concrete goal. That's the third Change Agent Essential: **Set a Concrete Goal.**

Chapter 8

● ● ●

CHECK FOR SETTLERS AND DRAW YOUR BOUNDARIES

*"One of the truisms is that people don't mind change,
they just don't want others to change them."*

— EDGAR SCHEIN

You're ready to drive change, you've overcome your excuses, and you want to start right away. You've drafted and shared your concrete goal. You want to act, move fast, and get results. I appreciate your energy, but I'll ask you to do two more planning steps before charging out to create your change: check for settlers and draw your change boundaries.

Settlers are the people who "live on the land" of your change, whose lives will be impacted by it.

Change Boundaries are the limits of your change, both now and in the future.

CHECK FOR SETTLERS

Because changes often aren't physical, it can be hard initially for change agents to picture whose lives are impacted by the change, who will witness the change and become curious, who will worry about the change, or who will rush to join it.

We must look for settlers because, though we rarely claim physical territory with our changes, we are often claiming organizational, community, or governmental territory that others think of as their own. Other metaphors are often used: rice bowls, turf, and domains. All are about possession and property rights to a place, process, or piece of space.

Many change agents I've encountered over the years, even in long-established organizations or communities, behave as though they are the first person to ever think of a change. If we borrow terms from urban planning, they are assuming their change will be built on a greenfield site, meaning a plot of land that has never been built on before.

I've often been the bearer of bad news that the change they are proposing is actually a brownfield—that is, a building on a place that *has* been built on before. I have to tell them that there have been several others before them who have attempted this change. Many change agents, upon hearing this news, have crossed their arms, made a grumpy face, and stomped off. I called after them, "Wait. Come back. That doesn't mean you have to give up."

This pressure to be first is amplified by organizational reward structures and journalistic methods whereby we only focus on the exceptional cases: the first, the last, the youngest, the oldest, the fastest (though not the slowest). Fueled by this desire to be exceptional, the would-be change agent charges forward, blind to anyone who has undertaken the change before, is still trying to do it, used to do it, or still hopes it can be done.

I learned of my own blindness and its cure through a program called Leadership Kitsap. At one of the leadership days, we learned, "Don't assume you are the first person to want to work on your project." We were encouraged to find others who were already working toward the very change we wanted to accomplish, whether helping children with special needs, fighting hunger, or improving community health.

The leaders in Leadership Kitsap knew that if you don't look for others before you start, you'll soon be fighting the other group for the local supply of donation dollars and public attention. The rivalry will hurt both groups, as well as the people they hope to serve. Overlap of effort creates the same pains within organizations.

Actually, it is worse inside organizations. It is worse because of the myth of perfect organizational design. The myth has people believing that the hierarchy laid out in organizational charts is a set of finely nested boxes without overlap or gap. It's pure myth because even a mild inspection finds many roles, tasks, and responsibilities that are duplicated, undone, or entirely unknown. If the myth were made visible, you would see an organization map that looks like early 18th century maps of continental North America. Whole sections would be blank space, speculation, or no-man's zones, while other areas would be so overpopulated that it would be hard to tell who owned what or who was responsible to whom.

Earlier I told the story of Lewis and Clark and the Corps of Discovery's trip west from St. Louis. Many know that story, but they may not know that the two captains carried a special order from President Jefferson to be opened only after they had passed the last known territory on the map. When Lewis and Clark opened the special order and read it to the Corps, they all learned they weren't just explorers, they were part of what we might call the first amazing race. President Jefferson presumed that the British had also dispatched a team on a race west to the Pacific coast. The captains and their corps expected to find a British flag and fort awaiting them along the shores of the Pacific, when and if they ever found those shores. They were surprised and overjoyed when they discovered they were the first explorers to reach the spot by land from the east.

The story is relevant to our work today as change agents, because if Lewis and Clark were expecting to find other competing explorers when they arrived at the Pacific, then we shouldn't be surprised to discover other similar groups in our organizations as we deploy our change efforts. When we start a new onboarding process for recent college graduates, for example, chances are good someone in Human Resources or Recruiting may take offense that we are appropriating their work. We should expect to find another volunteer group in our same city committed to solving Problem X, too. Unlike Lewis and Clark, we don't have to presume we are in true competition with these other people though.

If we can care more about our change than we care about being first, we can open ourselves up to the tasks of finding the settlers, then partnering with them or learning from them.

There are four categories of settlers that I encourage you to look for. Their category names and respective objections are:

- Current Settlers: "That change is my job."
- Missing Settlers: "That change is not my job."
- Past Settlers: "I did that change or tried to do it."
- Downstream Settlers: "Someone always does that job."

CURRENT SETTLERS

If you've tried to create changes before, you've likely encountered the first group of settlers, the current settlers who say, "That change is my job." These are the settlers who give rise to the meetings about "rice bowls" and "turf battles"—and who launch plans to reorganize the company, committees, or departments to "align authority and responsibility."

I've had change agents seek me out when they have encountered these settlers, wanting me to side with them against their (perceived) adversaries. The change agents are shocked when I side with the current settlers. To relieve their shock, I offer a simple analogy.

Imagine your change as the equivalent of barging into a settler's home and redecorating it without their permission. Often, this is how the settler perceives your change. If you did that, would you expect the person to be angry with you?

The settler might say, "Here I was, minding my own business, when Change Agent Z, broke into my world and started moving my stuff around, taking things I care about, and hiding other things from me. Then they told me I should like it or I'm the problem!"

We don't like it when other people barge into our space, so we shouldn't do it to them.

Now, you might say, "But it isn't always my change! Often I'm just following orders to implement a change." I understand, but that doesn't absolve you of your responsibility to treat the settlers with respect.

Ask to be invited into the settler's space. Don't barge in.

Have a mutual friend introduce you to them.

Never say, "I'm just doing my job!" That doesn't help.

Advocate for their concerns to whomever sent you.

Those are some ways to make the change go smoother, faster and more happily.

What you might learn from the current settlers is that your change's best path is *not* through the settler's territory—that it's actually best to go around it. Sometimes this deviation is to avoid the conflict. Other times it is best because the settler showed you a better route to your destination.

You may have been right initially when you assumed that your change's fastest route to success was directly through the settler's area of responsibility. You might find, however, that a slightly longer route actually produces an even better outcome, like a railroad skirting a hill instead of going over it.

I've found my best change partners in these current settlers. They are well established in their areas of responsibility, they know the terrain, and they have a network of connections. Furthermore, they have credibility and often, importantly, funding (or ways to get funding) for projects. Rather than build all of that infrastructure yourself, you can leverage the settlers' infrastructure by partnering with them. You'll go faster than you could alone.

SETTLER PARTNERSHIP SAVES SIX MONTHS

With our playground project, we didn't go alone. We found a settler and partnered instead. That one decision saved us six months or more of delay.

We knew that we would need a way to accept donations, and that would mean becoming a 501(c)3 organization, a designation named for the part of the U.S. tax code that governs charities. The typical timeline to 501(c)3 status is at least six months, sometimes much longer. We knew we wanted to move faster and we knew to check for settlers. So, we approached an established, well-respected organization in our community that had a charter to enable the best lives for children and adults with special needs. That organization was Holly Ridge Center.

We asked Roxanne Bryson, the executive director of Holly Ridge, if they would partner with us as our financial sponsor. We would then be able to get the benefit of their ability to take in and report our funding. Then, together we could turn the funding over to the City of Bremerton when it came time to buy the playground equipment.

Wonderfully, graciously, Roxanne said yes. Then, mere weeks after launching the playground project, we were collecting donations. It was phenomenal.

MISSING SETTLERS

Missing settlers are mysterious people that everyone else assumes are doing the change you are seeking. These are the settlers you are sent to find when you ask someone, "Is Change X your job?" and they say, "No. I think that is Person Z or Organization A's job."

You go forward to ask Person Z or someone in Organization A and both say, "We don't do that. We don't know who does. Try Person W or Organization B." And on and on you go, hunting for someone that doesn't exist.

My favorite missing settler checks are the ones where two groups point back at each other, but neither will claim responsibility. Group A says it is Group B's job. Group B says it is Group A's. You want to scream, "I don't care who's job it *should* be. I need to know whose job it *is*." Scream if you like, but you've been given a gift.

The gift is a kernel of knowledge that is hiding in plain sight—that everyone else is actually missing. No one is taking ownership of this space. What joy! What possibility! What will you do now with this unclaimed ground?

You may be thinking, "Finally, a green field where I can do anything I want." Nope. Close, though. You're less likely to have found a green field than a long-abandoned brown field. Your next task should be to seek out our third category of settlers, past settlers.

PAST SETTLERS

These past settlers are all the people who have tried to create your change before. I recommend starting with the people who have tried in the closest location or most similar organization to your current change.

That means looking for people in your own community or organization who have tried the change *before* you look for people further afield. I encourage you to start with proximity because your fellow community or organization members usually have more directly applicable information to your change—for example, physical limitations like budget rules or system capacities, key intelligence like the names of those who opposed or supported the change when they last tried—and much more.

You'll find these past settlers by asking around, "Who has tried Change X before?" or "Do you know anyone who has ever worked on Change X or something similar?" You'll want to ask the people who have been part of your organization or community for a while, the ones with big networks and long memories. They will be wells of information: who tried, what was the setting, how did it turn out, what is left of the change now.

I encourage all change agents to seek out these past settlers and to be bold about reaching out to them directly. Ask for a meeting. Set up a time for a coffee, tea, or beer (depending on your local custom) to get them talking about their attempt at your change. Tell them what you are working toward. and ask for their advice. Then, listen.

Listen well. Take notes. Ask follow-up questions that get beneath any vague comments like, "IT wouldn't let us." Ask, "Who in IT was opposed to the change?" If the past settler gives you a name, great. Is that person still with your IT organization? If they can't give you a name, then you know you are already further along on the journey than they achieved.

When you get further along the journey to your change than the expert that went before you, you will have encountered a situation that most American children of the 1980s know well from the movie *Goonies*. It's a Chester Copperpot moment. There's a time on the Goonies' quest for the treasure of the pirate One Eyed Willie when the Goonies find the body of the famed treasure hunter Chester Copperpot. Mikey, the group's *de facto* leader, rallies the Goonies to keep going, because they've already gotten further than the expert, Mr. Copperpot.

I'm going to encourage you to keep going with your change too. Just because others tried the change and didn't make it does not mean you should turn around. In fact, using all the best of what the past settlers achieved, you can now go farther.

Now that we've found the current, missing, and past settlers, we only have one more group of settlers to seek out—the downstream settlers.

DOWNSTREAM SETTLERS

The downstream settlers are the people who rely on what is happening today. If your change disrupts that flow, they will experience it eventually, though not immediately. This time lag, from the change to the time when the change will reach them, is why downstream settlers are so often not found until it's too late to help them live with the change.

A program is discontinued, and the change team and some settlers (the ones who were found) celebrate. Then a week, month, or year later, a downstream settler appears needing the discontinued program functionality. Often, the damage can't be undone, and the downstream settler suffers.

A world-class change agent, which I know you are or are on your way to becoming, will always discipline themselves to look for downstream settlers before launching a change. It is the right thing to do and ensures the greatest long term success for all.

The way to find these downstream settlers is first to ask, "Who relies on the current state?" and "Who will come looking for the current state if it's stopped?" Ask around. Ping your networks.

Finding downstream settlers is essential when your change permanently eliminates something (e.g., phasing out a program or discarding old equipment, tools, or processes). After the elimination, there is often no recovery method. Irreversible changes can have enormous organizational costs that downstream settlers will be forced to absorb. The costs and consequences can be mitigated.

A mitigation plan might include a place to store the remnants of the past state, or the data archive, for a set period of time (months or years), with a little note posted somewhere that says:

> "If you've found this note, it means you were looking for Information X. It is now at Location L. Contact Person P to access it.
>
> This notice is valid until Date D.
>
> If no one contacts Person P by Date D, Information X will be discarded."

Some people will see this mitigation planning as waste. They'll point to its costs. Compare the costs of mitigation to the potential costs to downstream settlers. Imagine who might arrive moments, days, or weeks later seeking a capability or information that cannot be recovered. What would it cost to recreate the capability or knowledge? What delays would the organization face?

In my experience, we don't capture those costs and delays on organizational balance sheets or government budgets, but we suffer the costs regardless. So, I encourage you strongly to seek out downstream settlers or plan for them even if you can't find them.

STAKEHOLDERS VERSUS SETTLERS

Traditional change management processes include steps to manage stakeholders. If you are familiar with these processes, you may have thought I mean stakeholders when I say settlers; I don't.

I have found that stakeholders and settlers are different, both in the actual people included in each group and in the way that change agents interact with them.

In traditional change management, the processes around stakeholder management focus on identifying the people who have a say in your change going forward—and in doing your due diligence to meet their needs. In theory, that approach is valid. In practice, I usually find change agents going through legalistic motions to fulfill an abstract obligation to the stakeholders, as they attempt to minimize the stakeholders' impact on the change. So too, stakeholders are usually seen as people with power over the change. They may be managers in other work groups. Or perhaps they are elected or appointed officials in various government departments or portions of the volunteer organization. Not often enough does stakeholders include the individuals who will actually be impacted by the change—the everyday people who must accept and adopt the change in order for it to flourish.

> *"Beware of the stakeholder who doesn't pay;*
> *he has no reason to compromise."*
>
> — NIELS MALOTAUX

Stakeholder management processes often give control over a change to a range of officials who might have an interest in the change but who do not have to alter their own behavior or processes to see the change implemented. This control slows change and frustrates change agents. It's into this frustration that I inject settlers as an alternative or compliment to stakeholders.

DRAW YOUR BOUNDARIES

After you've found all the settlers and partnered with some of them, now you must draw your change boundaries.

Change Boundaries are the limits of your change, both now and in the future. They help settlers, from both the present and the future, determine whether you are a friend or foe, whether they should find you now or wait, and whether to help you or hurt you.

When you propose your change, you'll declare your concrete goal. You'll think you are talking about right now. You are. However, the people who hear about your change won't just be thinking about right now. They'll be thinking, "The change agent's goal now is their concrete goal. But what is their future goal?"

They won't be asking you these questions. They'll be thinking them and answering them for themselves based on their past experiences. If you could listen to their thoughts, you would hear something like this:

I'm Person X.

I've experienced a lot of changes where some Change Agent A said, "I plan to try out Process C with Small Group G."

Quickly, Change Agent A or Senior Manager Z pushed to implement Process C on everyone, including me.

I know you are Change Agent B, and I heard you say your goal now is "Try out Process D only with Group E," but I know your future goal is world domination!

I must either stop you or "fix" your change now, while I still can!

WORLD DOMINATION

Faced with the threat of world domination, which is much harder to fight than a local implementation, Person X will feel compelled to crush you and your concrete goal before you can achieve your first success. Or, Person X will attempt to take over your change and load you up with all the change features they want until you're swamped and cannot continue.

This is a learned behavior Person X has acquired from years of being forced to implement change after change—changes that failed to take into account the special situations that Person X faced. Expecting Person

X to embrace your change without variability is the equivalent of designing a t-shirt to fit an "average" man and then expecting everyone globally to wear the shirt.

If we had to walk into work or around our communities and see all people, small and large, men, women and children all struggling to wear the same size clothing, we would be shocked by our own stupidity. Most universally-applied, standardized changes fit about as well, but we don't see the consequences of the poor fit. People like Person X feel the consequences, though, and they don't want the consequences repeated.

You can prevent the one-size-fits-few frustrations, along with the justified attacks on you and your change, by drawing your change boundaries. The change boundaries are a declaration of intent so that the people encountering your change are not forced to make their own assumptions.

We encountered this change boundary confusion with the playground project. We had been working for years to raise money and build one beyond accessible playground at Evergreen Rotary Park in the city of Bremerton, Washington. We were asked by the county parks board to meet with them to describe our project. We were proud of the project and happy to share the lessons we had learned, so we jumped at the chance to present to the county.

During the meeting, someone from the county group asked whether we would like to partner with them too. In general, we liked "partnering," so that sounded like a good idea—but then I thought, "What do they mean by partnering?" So I asked. It turned out their definition of partnership was for us to raise money for them for a playground too.

My response was swift, "Oh. No. Our goal now is to build the playground in Bremerton. Our future goal is to rest." It was at that moment that the clarity of change boundaries was brought home for me. Most groups who are successful go on to expand their success to the area around them, be that from a work group to an organization, or a community to a county, a state or beyond. Since most people don't stop at their initial success, we had to declare our change boundary or we would be communicating a message we did not intend.

Now, in our case, the county's assumption of our expanding to county domination of accessible playgrounds was not a threat to their authority. Therefore, they supported it. Their assumption was, nonetheless, incorrect. I'm convinced that if we had accepted the expansion before we had finished building our first playground, we would have divided our attention, confused our donors, and squandered the last of our remaining energy for the change.

WAITING FOR A CHANGE THAT NEVER COMES

Without clear change boundaries, you'll also find others waiting around patiently for your change to come to them. They suffer while waiting for you to get to them, even though you never intended to do so. Again, this is a failure on their part to assume a future goal that you didn't intend. They assumed that after your now goal, your concrete goal, then your future goal would be:

Provide the concrete goal to Person X or Group Z.

The damage, when others assume your future goal is to provide the concrete goal for them, is that they will not attempt the concrete goal for themselves. This situation happens frequently in organization and communities.

A group of volunteers goes to a village to build a safe drinking water supply. People in the next village assume that the volunteers will be back the next summer to build them a safe water supply too. If the villagers don't check their assumption, and wait rather than finding volunteers to partner with them, it is likely that no volunteers will ever arrive in their village.

In organizations, this situation manifests itself as a program rollout at the corporate headquarters to develop a certain group of people in a specific competency. People at the field offices wait patiently for the headquarters program to expand to the field. It never does. The field employees could have launched their own program to gain the competency, but instead they waited, because they assumed wrongly that the future goal would entail giving the program to them.

If you're currently caught in this situation and are waiting for a change to arrive, quit assuming you are the future goal. Ask, and act. If you are driving a change, be clear what your future goal will be. You will save others years of waiting around you.

THREE PLAYGROUNDS INSTEAD OF ONE

During the playground project we clarified our change boundaries, telling anyone and everyone that our goal now was building our playground at Evergreen Rotary Park in Bremerton, Washington; and our future goal was to rest. Then, we met two groups who chose to start their own accessible playground projects, one to the north of our location and one to the south.

No one asked, "Did you know Person Y is doing the same thing as you? What are you going to do about it?" Instead, we got comments like, "Isn't it fantastic that Group A is creating a playground too?"

We could confidently answer, "Yes. Yes, it is great. We're excited for them and love sharing with them the lessons we've learned."

Today, the children and adults with special needs in Kitsap County, Washington have three accessible play locations instead of zero or only one. That is a change that continues to transform lives.

MAP THE TERRAIN

When you've both checked for settlers and drawn your change boundaries, you've effectively mapped your change terrain. This map ensures that you, as well as everyone tangentially associated with your change, will know where you are, where you are going, and how to find you. It also ensures that everyone involved will have a clear idea of what your change means now and what it will mean in the future. This is a minimal, essential context that enables successful change. Hence, the fourth Change Agent Essential is: **Map the Terrain**.

Part 3

ACTING

"...[B]ut by acting as if I were not afraid
I gradually ceased to be afraid."

— *Theodore Roosevelt*

D o you think change takes time? Usually, when people say a change will "take time," they mean months at best, years typically, and sometimes decades or lifetimes.

Bah! I think we all suffer from diminished expectations. We can do better. Though we may have accepted glacial rates of change in the past, such low expectations do not have to shape our future.

When we compare just the first four of seven Change Agent Essentials to status-quo change projects, we can see a stark difference in tactics. The tactics that flow out of the Change Agent Essentials lead not only to more unified teams and more effective processes—but also to far quicker paths to change.

I know you can drive the change you want today and achieve results faster than you've ever experienced and faster than anyone ever expected. But, you'll have to break from the status quo.

You will have to act differently. That is easy to say, but difficult to do. Until now we've been talking about what actions you might take. Now, it is time to *act*.

Chapter 9

●　　●　　●

WALK YOUR OWN WAY

*"Improvement is doubly difficult when individual
habit is reinforced by group inertia."*

— United States Navy Correspondence Manual

THEODORE ROOSEVELT MILLS

When I was sixteen weeks pregnant with our second child, my husband and I learned that our baby would be born with a common birth defect, spina bifida. Our baby, a son, had an opening in his spinal column just above his tailbone, and a portion of his spinal nerves were protruding from his spine into a cyst that had formed on his back. The neurosurgeon told us our son would never walk.

My husband and I chose to give our small, weak boy a strong name to embed courage in him to overcome the obstacles that were already in his way. We named him Theodore Roosevelt Mills. Theodore Roosevelt was not only the 26th President of the United States, but also a historically successful change agent, and before that a boy who overcame his own weak body.

When Theodore Roosevelt was young, he was beset with asthma. His condition weakened him, and his parents regularly feared they would lose their son to his frequent breathing challenges. Historians and biographers tell a story of Roosevelt's father, also named Theodore, sitting on his young son's bed and challenging the boy to remake his weak body. Edmund Morris retells the story in *The Rise of Theodore Roosevelt*:

> "'Theodore,' the big man said..., 'you have the mind but you have not the body, and without the help of the body the mind cannot go as far as it should. You must make your body. It is hard drudgery to make one's body, but I know you will do it.'"

It was with that story in mind that we named our son.

Fast forward nearly four years from that first day when we were told our Theodore would never walk. In the intervening years, Theodore, my husband, and I had persevered through bracing and stretching, therapy, casts, and surgeries to enable Theodore to walk. When he was three years old, Theodore finally walked, but only with the help of a heavy metal walker. He could pull it behind him on smooth surfaces for short distances. It was exhausting, limited, and slow. This was not good enough for a tough-minded little boy. He wanted to go faster.

Theodore worked on his balance. He worked on his strength. Finally, he graduated from the heavy walker to light forearm crutches that allowed him to travel faster, farther, and across uneven ground. On a warm August day in 2011, Theodore (on his new crutches) came with me to the county fair to watch a friend's daughter sing.

THEODORE AT THE COUNTY FAIR

Now, you can imagine that a boy not quite four years old doesn't want to watch a teenage girl sing when there are all the other county fair attractions to look at. No. He wanted to go see the cows in the barn across the grassy field from the performance stage.

As a mother who wants to raise a strong, independent son, I let Theodore get down from the bleachers and wander off on his crutches toward the cow barn. When he was about 30 feet away, I took this photo of him proudly walking off toward his goal.

Then, I watched as a fascinating thing happened. The small crowd gathered near the stage began to notice this little boy with obvious differences wandering off unaccompanied. Many began to stretch their arms out wide, even though they weren't close to Theodore. They hoped, I suppose, to protect him from some imagined danger. As Theodore continued his steady progress toward the barn, a number of other people in the crowd began to jerk their heads to the left and the right, looking around wildly.

I could see the thought in their eyes, "Where is this child's mother?" (Isn't it funny that people never seem to wonder where a wandering young child's father is?)

As I observed the body language of the people around me, I was struck by the two very different reactions. Those with outstretched arms seemed to want to rescue Theodore from the obvious exertion that walking required. He was wobbly. He was slow, compared to others (though for Theodore, the pace was strong and fast). These onlookers seemed to be restraining themselves from running over to him, scooping him up in their arms, and saying, "Precious angel, just tell me where you want to go and I'll take you there. No need for your to worry or struggle. I can do it for you."

The others, the ones frowning as they looked around in every direction, seemed to be having an opposite reaction. I mentioned the questioning look of "Where is this child's mother?" Within moments that puzzlement expanded to include expressions of frustration and disdain. These people seemed angry that I wasn't hovering over Theodore. Angry that I hadn't prevented him from trying. Angry that he was loose and uncontrolled, at least from their perspective.

From Theodore's perspective and mine, he was finally free. Something his peers had been able to do for years, run off a bit from mom to explore, he was finally getting to do. My boy was learning and growing, and I wanted to support that growth. He remained always within my sight and always safe, but he was also independent and increasingly confident as he went. That's what he and I were both seeking, whether these other people around us understood it or not.

I share this story with you because when you first act to drive change instead of driving people, you will be looked at much as Theodore was that day. If you send an optional meeting notice, start with your passion for a change, and ask others to partner with you. Most of the people around you will look at you funny. They will think you've lost all your strength, gone wobbly, gone slow, and need to be saved or stopped.

I've seen change agents who begin to drive change encounter well-meaning managers or officials who say, "You don't need to ask people to attend your meetings. I'll just tell them they have to attend or else." You'll have to stop them before they *drive people* on your behalf. It will happen. Be ready.

Alternatively, you might encounter people who will be confused by the leadership you take toward change. They will ask you questions like, "Who told you to do this?" and "Is this your job?" Those questions are the equivalent of asking, "Where is your mother, and why did she let you out of her sight?" Feel free to tell them, if you like, that I told you to go toward the change you desired. They can take their concerns up with me. I don't mind. My contact information is at the back of this book. I welcome their emails.

As I've sent change agents out into the world, strong in driving change (but noticeably different from those around them), many have found strength in Theodore's story. They've come back to me and said, "I was in a meeting and it was just like Theodore at the fair. They tried to drive people. I said no thanks. I was driving change. It is working."

Driving change is different from the status quo of driving people, but it doesn't have to remain simply an alternative methodology. It can (and should) become your new normal. When I first learned that Theodore had spina bifida, my doctor put the news into perspective. He said, "You have a new normal," and went on to explain what normal often looks like for a child with spina bifida. Today, almost nine years later, I can say with certainty that he was right.

Ted, as he likes to be called, is a strong boy, strong in his own way. He makes his way in the world in the manner that works best for him—and you can too.

Why not try?

YOUR NEW NORMAL

Many leadership books say some version of, "To succeed in change or in leadership, a leader must walk their talk." In our context of driving change, walking the talk means always, without fail, driving change and not people. Acting on this imperative will be harder than it sounds. Old habits are hard to break.

People will tell you that you can't drive change. Don't believe them. My husband and I didn't believe Theodore's doctor when he said our child would never walk. Ted defies that claim every day. You can drive your change without anyone else's permission. Drive your change, and prove them all wrong.

It's hard to be different when nearly everyone else is following the status quo. You'll be pressured to drive people, yet you can resist. You *can* drive change.

When you drive change, you'll be challenging the firmly held assumptions of others that you must be in a position of authority before you can lead. You'll be defying the conventional wisdom that you must drive people, and that the bigger and vaguer the change, the better.

We can't expect others to do something that we're not willing to do ourselves. So, now, we must challenge your firmly held assumptions about others.

Chapter 10

• • •

CHALLENGE YOUR ASSUMPTIONS

*"...[M]isunderstandings and neglect create more
confusion in this world than trickery and malice. At any
rate, the last two are certainly much less frequent."*

— JOHANN WOLFGANG VON GOETHE

W e assume we can do much less than we can, while at the same time assuming that others can do much more than they really can. To get better, faster change results, we must reverse these assumptions. We must harness our own power, while giving others grace as they try to harness their power too.

In this chapter, I'll outline several more assumptions that must be challenged before we can get our best change results in partnership, rather than competition, with the people most affected. These assumptions are adapted to our change context from an excellent work on defeating defensive routines in the workplace, *Discussing the Undiscussable* by William Noonan.

Everyone hates change. That's an assumption many people hold. It is a false assumption, but it's one that is repeated over and over again as though it is true. Why is this? It is, I believe because if everyone truly does hate change, then I am justified in doing nothing—or, worse, I am justified in driving people. If they are going to hate it anyway, I might as well just force them, right? Wrong.

Your next step on your change journey is to challenge your assumptions about the people surrounding your change. By challenging your own assumptions—an action you can take without any help from the other people—you can move closer to winning others to your change. And, you'll do it faster than you've ever experienced.

THEIR PERSPECTIVE IS VALID

The first assumption to challenge is that only *your* perspective is valid. When we get passionate about our change, we often develop change blindness, believing that anyone who doesn't avidly support our change is against it (and us). This mindset, which turns all indifferent and oppositional people into enemies, slows our change.

We can replace this assumption with a short statement: "Their perspective is valid." In other words, we affirm that people who oppose our change have good reasons to do so—and we remind ourselves to listen to their concerns. In listening, we show our respect, while at the same time gaining information we can use to help our change succeed.

We shouldn't be seeking others' perspectives in order to undermine them. We do not say, "Their perspective is as valid as mine," implying some equation that must balance. We acknowledge their right to have their perspective, absent any equivalence we might be tempted to attach.

Even when change agents are willing to entertain the idea that others have valid perspectives, I find they sometimes isolate themselves and their change teams into meetings to diligently presume what the change conscripts might accept as valid answers to the "what's in it for the change conscript?" question. It may only be my perspective, but these meetings seem like wastes of time.

If we knew the perspectives of others so well, why would even need to hold these meetings? Wouldn't we have simply included their concerns in the first design?

I find these meetings are usually about further justifying to ourselves that we are the only ones who have the best interests of the Group A in mind, and applauding ourselves for creating such a compelling change. So compelling, in fact, that Persons X, Y, and Z will either adopt it quickly or be forced to reveal to all that they don't really care about the success of Group A. Does this line of thinking sound like an assumption that Persons X, Y, and Z have valid perspectives? No? I didn't think so.

TACTIC: CHANGE PERSPECTIVES AND DISSOLVE RESISTANCE

Instead, I encourage you to try a quick five-step method I call Change Perspectives and Dissolve Resistance.

> **Step 1:** Invite all the people affected by the change (or their representatives) to a meeting place (either virtual or physical). Thank them for attending, and let them know you intend to take action based on what they share.

> **Step 2:** Create four categories of input, typically represented as a 2×2 matrix. The categories are Positive Effects of the Change, Negative Effects of the Change, Positive Effects of Not Changing, Negative Effects of Not Changing.

Step 3: Give everyone sticky notes or their own separate electronic space to write their thoughts. Then ask them to silently and independently write the effects of the change from their perspective for each of the categories. They can have many effects associated with each category or none for some of the categories.

Step 4: Have everyone post their effects onto a common board.

Step 5: Those who want to remain and work towards a win-win solution for all are asked to stay, review the shared information, and suggest improvements to the change that would result in win-win features.

This five-step process can take as little as 20 minutes or as long as a day. It depends on how many people are involved, how challenging the change is, and how creative the win-win solution designers are willing to be. The only pre-work is deciding who will get a voice by planning and issuing the invitations to the exercise.

WE ARE ONLY SEEING PIECES OF THE WHOLE

The next assumption change agents typically fall into is believing that they are seeing the whole situation impacted by the change. If we don't challenge this assumption, we often create problems for others while we try to solve our own problems.

We cut Program A to reduce the budget of Group A only to cause Group B to have to add Program B to handle what Program A used to do—usually at higher cost and lower quality.

We add Feature C to Change X because we love it and we convinced Group C to love it too. But, it delays Change X, and Group D is hurt by the delay.

The antidote to charging forward with our change without understanding the larger, systemic consequences is to pause before we act, remembering that we are seeing only a piece of the whole.

This is not a new assumption for change agents to overcome. There is the ancient parable of the blind men and the elephant, where each man feels a part of the elephant, declaring what he believes it to be. As a group, all of the blind men miss the bigger connection of every piece to the same elephant.

Plenty of changes I've encountered, if translated back into the elephant problem, ended up as grotesque constructions of an elephant with three tails and no trunk, or four tails. The change efforts became so deformed because these odd constructions were the only ones all parties would agree to support. Such monstrosities are unnecessary, though—if only we will challenge our assumption and open our eyes to the existence of a greater whole.

OTHERS HAVE POSITIVE INTENTIONS

When changes are rolling through an organization, they regularly create negative consequences for some group of people. These negative consequences are due in part to incomplete settler checks, or an absence of any settler check. They are also due to the size of most changes that are unleashed into systems—large-scale, one-size-fits-few changes that we've talked about in a previous chapter.

Have you ever suffered the consequences of these large changes? Have you lost Feature X, Program Y, Capability Z to budget cuts? Have you been forced to accept conditions that you consider unreasonable, unacceptable, and unforgivable? Have you felt like a little bunny run over by a large delivery truck? You're not alone.

Over the years, I've been called in time and time again to play medic to those injured by large, one-size-fits-few changes. The injured have regularly begged me to get them justice for their suffering. They wanted public apologies, change reversals, resignations of those they considered the evildoers. They railed against those who (they believed) hurt them intentionally with the change.

They were shocked when I refused to hate, refused to attack, and refused to retaliate. But, my refusals came from a belief in the following assumption: Those responsible for the damage and injury had positive intentions.

They, the people who hurt others with their change, rarely ever intend to hurt others. In fact, most of the time, they are entirely unaware of the negative consequences they inflicted through their change. Those who do understand the costs often feel the consequences are justified by the necessity of the change. These conclusions are hard to hear, but they are also entirely reasonable.

They are reasonable because often the people driving these large, one-size-fits-few changes, are simply stuck in the status-quo patterns of driving people, failing to check for settlers and making the change bigger than it needs to be. They are the change equivalent of a delivery truck rushing between delivery stops. When one of these trucks accidentally hits a bird or little rabbit, they don't stop to mourn. They keep going.

This is understandable for the truck driver, but it is nonetheless death for the bird or rabbit. If we (or our colleagues) are the run-over bird or rabbit in the analogy, our trauma is very real—yet we cannot logically blame the truck driver for doing his or her job.

In changes, we serve ourselves and our fellow change agents better when we assume that others are trying to create the best change they can, and when their change hurts us it is accidental rather than purposeful. With this mindset, we are free to reach out to them, explain the consequences, and ask to partner with them to remove or mitigate the negative effects. They'll likely be confused at first when you ask to partner instead of retaliating or pouting, but if you ask enough times, most of your fellow change agents will come around. If they don't, then (unfortunately), you've found those few malicious tricksters about whom Goethe wrote.

WE MUST TAKE RESPONSIBILITY FOR UNINTENDED CONSEQUENCES

Finally, should we create our change and learn that, despite our best efforts, we have inflicted some injury, the right answer is not to say, "I didn't mean to," and walk way.

No. The right answer is to apologize for the unintended consequence and partner with the injured person to remedy it. We must be ready to do this because, even when we have the best of intentions, our solutions will sometimes create bigger problems.

The theme of "best intentions lead to bigger problems" is highlighted in a concept called the "cobra effect." The story which gives the concept its name may be apocryphal, but real-life examples of the cobra effect abound. Generically, we could describe the cobra effect this way:

Organization A thinks the world would be better with fewer Object Xs.

Organization A rewards anyone for finding (and sometimes also for destroying) an Object X.

The reward is so appealing that people begin to create Object Xs only to then find and destroy them for the reward.

Organization A cancels the reward, but there is a delay before people realize to stop creating Object Xs.

The world is left with more Object Xs.

Some stories tell of cobras in India, others of rats in Vietnam. I've even heard the story told about bugs in software.

When software developers were paid for finding bugs in their software—shock of all shocks—bugs went up. When the payments for bugs got too high, the program was cancelled; or so the story goes.

Not every change reaches its intended outcome without unintended negative consequences. When you are surprised by a bad outcome to your well-intended solution, my recommendation is, first, to apologize. Then, do what you can, in partnership with those who brought the situation to your attention, to eliminate the unintended consequences.

CHALLENGE ASSUMPTIONS

When we walk our own way, challenging others assumptions of what we can and can't do and how we can and can't do it, and we are willing to challenge our assumptions of others, we are living the fifth Change Agent Essential: **Challenge Assumptions**.

Chapter 11

● ● ●

FOCUS ON SUSTAINMENT

"Changes in a work group, a division, or an entire company can come undone, even after years of effort, because the new approaches haven't been anchored firmly...."

— JOHN KOTTER

Like a warm cup of coffee that cools in a cold room unless left on a warmer, so too a change fades amidst the cool of the status quo unless energy is applied to sustain it.

This reality is hard to face for many change agents. They've been conditioned through driving people to focus on launching the change, not sustaining it. When you're driving people, if the change fades, it is the fault of those other people. When you're driving change, you're forced to confront the reality that was there the whole time: Without energy invested to sustain a change, it will fade.

If we revisit the change paths we covered in Chapter 3, we see that since so few changes created by driving people ever reach the goal, it is not surprising that many of us lack practice in sustaining change.

When we dedicate ourselves to driving change, we have a better chance of reaching our goal, but if we revert to our old behaviors and walk away once the goal is attained, we'll find the change energy falls with our departure—and the change outcome disappears.

I think this tendency to walk away, even when we succeed, is fed by a focus on completing the change task instead of sustaining the results. Even when change agents win, we are prone accidentally to drop the change too soon.

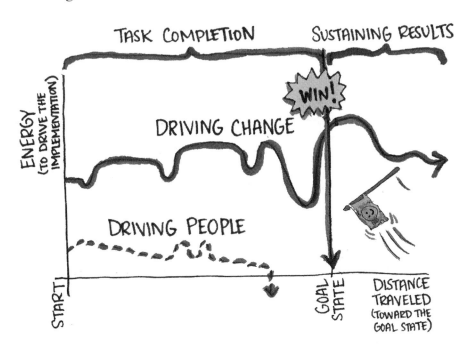

WHEN WE FOCUS ON TASK COMPLETION

Chances are good you've been part of one of these win-then-drop changes. You've issued Policy A, launched Product B, built Location C. You've worked hard. You're proud of what you've accomplished. Then, with the task complete, you walk away or you are reassigned to a new project. When you return a week, a month, or a year later, what do you find? Lack of use? Low revenue? Deterioration?

When we focus only on task completion, it is as though all our change effort was for nothing. The energy drops with our departure, and the change dies. These change deaths are preventable if only we will shift our focus toward sustainment.

WHEN WE FOCUS ON SUSTAINMENT

When we shift our attention from task completion to sustainment, we have the opportunity not just to succeed at our change, but also to succeed in changing our organizations, communities, nations, and world.

John Kotter found a pattern in unsuccessful changes of a lack of sustainment, and he therefore devoted the final two steps in his eight-step process to sustainment. Step 7 was, "Consolidating Gains and Producing More Change," and Step 8 was, "Anchoring New Approaches in the Culture."

Kotter knew and shared the importance of sticking with the change past the initial joy of the win of implementation or launch. Without the discipline of sustainment, the data told him, old habits creep quickly back in, and the superficial change implementations crack and fall away. My experience as a practitioner and consultant attests to the truth of Kotter's findings.

Sustainment requires a plan tailored to your specific change and environment. What plan is best? It depends.

Some change agents cultivate sustainment partners, people in authority positions who can staff and fund the ongoing aspects of the change.

SUSTAINING THE PLAYGROUND

For the playground project, our sustainment partner was the local parks and recreation department. After our playground was built, the parks department became responsible for ongoing maintenance. It was now their playground too. To support their sustainment, we designed the playground for minimal maintenance and gave the city funds to cover initial and ongoing costs.

Municipal projects often fail when it comes to this final step of long-term sustainment. After the hard work of fundraising to build the project ends, it often turns out that little consideration has been given to design or funding for maintenance. And, all too often, the energy dies before an endowment can be funded to sustain the project. We can, and should, do better.

SUSTAINABLE CHANGE BUFFERS

When your change depends on a change buffer to get it to the goal, you'll need to plan for sustainment of the change buffer after the win. I've seen many cases where policy exceptions were approved only until the effectiveness of the change could be proven. After the policy exception was revoked, the change quickly failed under the weight of the old system.

It's likely that if you needed the change buffer to launch the change you will need it throughout its implementation and sustainment. I encourage you to negotiate the change buffer to prove the concept of the change, then negotiate a lasting change buffer before you consider your work as a change agent done.

Some changes will require more than a change buffer. Change buffers typically allow the changed space to be different while all the others within the system remain the same. Some changes, however, require a full change in the larger system in order to succeed long-term. The magnitude of the sustainment needed shouldn't deter you from starting your change; however, you should take into account the amount of work still to be done after reaching your initial goal.

Once a change, within the buffer, has proven successful, your next step should center on buffer strengthening before moving on to expanding the change further out into the status quo. Buffer strengthening includes shifting from a personal buffer to a leadership buffer, winning an authority figure to your change via your results. Or, it could be shifting from a leadership buffer to a policy buffer, leveraging the leader's authority to publish a policy that makes your change an officially acceptable practice. These buffer-strengthening steps make your change more resilient amidst the often harsh conditions of the status quo.

Some change agents sustain their change by testing it as a manual process, then quickly working to implement it as an automatic function of the larger system. Whenever you can automate, you can set your change as a default in the system. Building in automatic process is like casting a spell of relative invisibility over the change. Whenever a person must actively sustain the change, it is easier to find, but when the day-to-day function of the larger system masks the automated change, it hides in plain sight. When you want to implement an automatic function, a great software designer or controls engineer is an asset on your change team. They will help you build in automatic sustainment from the beginning.

Regardless of how great your planning for sustainment, the energy in your change will wane over time. Consider how long your change must survive if it is to serve its purpose. Perhaps it doesn't need to stand like a Norman castle, but rather a nice country house, a good barn at a local farm, or a tent for a weekend of camping.

This reality of necessary and predicted timespan will allow you to choose the materials from which to build your change, Those materials may consist of policy or legal methods, actual building materials, software or hardware aspects, etc. Selecting the right materials usually requires bit of skilled engineering on top of good change agency. Feel free to gather a few experts that support your change to help you with these design trade-offs. You'll be glad you did.

Finally, as you plan for sustainment, don't forget the fundamentals that keep a change alive: people who continue to care about it, structures or organizations that reinforce it, funding that continues to enable it, and an authority that accepts ownership of it. These sustainment guardians, no matter what form they take, form the core of a sustainment system for any change. They keep the focus on sustaining your change. Hence, the sixth Change Agent Essential is: **Focus on Sustainment**.

Part 4

● ● ●

LEADING

"Our deepest fear is not that we are inadequate. Our deepest fear is that we are powerful beyond measure. It is our light, not our darkness that most frightens us....It's not just in some of us; it's in everyone and as we let our own light shine, we unconsciously give other people permission to do the same. As we are liberated from our own fear, our presence automatically liberates others."

— Marianne Williamson

The core problem we face is not a shortage of leadership. It is a shortage of belief.

You are a leader. You can lead. Believe it.

You can start the path that leads to changes that are better, faster, safer, and happier for you and those around you.

Overcoming the belief shortage requires you to stop pinning your hopes on others and instead start all changes with yourself.

Discover first. Plan first. Act first. Lead first.

The world is waiting for you. Believe it.

Why not try?

Now's your time to shine.

Chapter 12

● ● ●

ACCEPT YOUR CALL TO ACTION

"The supply of words in the world market is plentiful but the demand is falling. Let deeds follow words now."

—— LECH WAŁĘSA

CLIMB A FENCE AND CHANGE THE WORLD

In the late morning of August 14, 1980, an unemployed 36-year-old electrician climbed over the fence around the Lenin Shipyard in Gdansk, Poland, so he could support his friends inside. His friends were part of an ongoing labor dispute against the Soviet authorities running the shipyard. The man's name was Lech Wałęsa.

Wałęsa knew the risks he was taking. A decade earlier, 38 of his fellow shipyard workers had been shot and killed during strikes at the shipyard. And Wałęsa was hated by the Soviet shipyard bosses: he had been fired four years earlier for supporting unionizing activities and advocating for a monument to honor his fallen brethren. Yet, despite the grave risks, Wałęsa climbed over that fence.

Inside, he and his fellow union leaders gathered the support of the workers and created the trade union Solidarity. Maybe Wałęsa asked himself, "Who am I to lead this change?" But if he did, he didn't let such doubts stop him. He acted, led, risked, and created the change he wanted. He and the members of Solidarity truly changed the world.

Feel free to use his example to give you courage to risk and try too. Chances are good the risks you'll face aren't as menacing. Yes, the mayor might be upset with you. Yes, your boss's peer might not like your change. Those are real risks. I know, however, that if you are willing to face them, you can do wonderful and powerful things. Are you willing to risk, act, lead, and try, so that you can, like Wałęsa, create the change you seek?

FINDING THE COURAGE TO ACT

In June, 2015, I had the great privilege to speak from the stage at the European Solidarity Center in Gdansk, Poland. The European Solidarity Center is built on a portion of the former Lenin Shipyard. It sits just behind the shipyard gate Lech Wałęsa climbed over that now-famous August day. The setting stirred a storm of emotions for me as a change agent, former naval shipyard worker, and former union officer too.

I am in awe of the courage Wałęsa and his fellow workers demonstrated in standing up for workers' rights and fighting over the next decade for greater freedom. The struggle claimed lives, renewed lives, enriched lives, and forever changed the world. The Polish Solidarity activists are a testament to what people can do when they choose to lead and drive change.

CONFIDENCE IN YOU AND YOUR CHANGE

I wrote *Everyone is a Change Agent* to help you see that you can do wonderful and powerful things. I wrote it to help you see that you have a light that deserves to shine in the world—and that you can believe in yourself, discover your strength, plan, act, and lead, and remove the obstacles so others can follow.

My experience tells me that if I challenge you and stress you only a little, you'll read *Everyone is a Change Agent* and go right back to driving people or waiting for others to create the change you desire. In engineering terms, that's known as *elastic deformation*. You've stretched, but then you snap back to your old, comfortable ways.

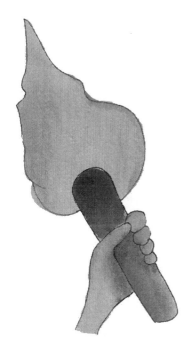

If I want to provoke lasting change in you, I need to push you, I need to challenge you, just past that point where you cannot be the same again. That is what is known as the *plastic deformation range*. The illustrations, terms, and stories of this book were designed to plastically deform your idea of change. The next time you enter into a conversation about a change, I suspect you'll make mental notes to yourself as you hear statements affirming status-quo tactics.

"Ah," you'll think, "this person is trying to drive people."

When you watch the news and want to cry out, "Someone should do something!" you'll remember the exhortation you heard in the pages of this book:

"You're someone! You can do something! You can do what you can, with what you have, where you are. Why not try?"

You can do it. Believe it.

Believe in you. I do.

A PATH WELL WORN

I'm not asking you to do something I haven't done. I've gone ahead of you down the driving change path. I've struggled, tripped, fallen onto the rocks, scraped my knees, then stood up and scaled obstacles people told me were impossible to conquer. So far, by the grace of God, I've overcome them all. The wisdom I offer here about change has come at great cost. If I've shared it in this book, I have done it, studied it, engineered it, tried to perfect it or break it, and tried again. It's taken me years to get this far, and I'm still learning.

Long ago, I made a fundamental shift in the way I approached change efforts in my work with other people. I began, as I have documented in previous chapters, consistently to drive change rather than people. Only recently did I realize, however, that when the change was personal I was still driving people—well, one person—*me*.

I would yell at myself, create lists and tasks for myself, and push myself to near exhaustion, offering punishments or rewards for complying with my self-imposed mandates. Then one day, I realized what I was doing—and I stopped.

Today, I drive change in my personal life in the same way as I drive change in my professional career and community life. I focus on the change and clear the obstacles that stand in my way. A simple example is how I recently created a gym kit of makeup and supplies to overcome my obstacle of "packing and unpacking my gym bag every day will take too long." Once I focused on the change and challenged myself to describe my obstacle, it was easier to change. I've found it is often small, not big, obstacles that stop changes, even changes in our own lives.

WHY NOT TRY?

You are your change advantage. You don't have to wait for others to change first. You can be the example, the leader, the light that others follow into the unknown. Who are you not to be?

You are outfitted with the Change Agent Essentials.

You are enough. You are ready.

Why not try?

Let our deeds, as Wałęsa encourages, now follow our words. Let our actions bring the change we desire into our lives. Let our commitment to living our values empower us toward driving change and helping others to do the same.

Let our choice to lead enable us and others to achieve lives filled with accomplishment, enthusiasm, and joy. Thus our seventh, and final, Change Agent Essential is just one word: **Try**.

Chapter 13

● ● ●

CALL OTHERS TO DRIVE CHANGE WITH YOU

"If your actions inspire others to dream more, learn more, and become more, you are a leader."

— JOHN QUINCY ADAMS

You don't have to be in a position of authority to create change. But, if you do have formal authority, you have a huge opportunity. Authority is an amplifier. If you use the Change Agent Essentials, your words and deeds will spread quickly throughout your sphere of authority. With great power comes great responsibility. Authority or not, do not delay.

TACTIC: ACT BEFORE YOU ASK

The most powerful action anyone with formal authority can do is to go first into any change: Act before you ask.

I am an authority figure.

I want Change C implemented.

I have acted to implement Change C in my life or work.

Now, I tell you what I've done to implement Change C.

I ask you to join me or tell me what obstacles prevent you from implementing Change C too.

TACTIC: PARTNER TO CLEAR OBSTACLES

Say the word "empowerment" to people, and often they'll wince and pull away, revealing deep change scars. In *Heart of Change*, John Kotter stated, "…[E]mpowerment is not about giving people new authority and new responsibilities and then walking away. It is all about removing barriers."

In my experience, people don't want their authority figures to force them to fend for themselves while they create change. They want their authority figures to join them, partnering to move the obstacles that are too heavy for them to overcome alone.

Don't believe the myth that authority figures shouldn't meddle in the changes their people are driving. Certainly, those you lead don't want you to drive them to change. They do, however, want you to enable them: through your presence (at times) and also through your capacity to marshal budgets, resources, and information in service of their change.

TACTIC: MODEL AND TEACH

You can quickly expand the change capabilities of the people within your sphere of authority if you model the Change Agent Essentials and describe what you are doing and why you are doing it.

Remind your team often that what propels your change is your choice to use the Change Agent Essentials, not your authority.

Leverage all the tactics available to you to model, teach, inform, and reinforce the Change Agent Essentials methodology of creating change. When you stumble and drive people (which you *will* do), admit your error, apologize, and begin once again to drive change. I've seen it many times; your people will follow your example.

TACTIC: PROTECT THEM AS THEY TRY

You can establish a leadership buffer that allows anyone within it to drive change, without question. You can set the example by implementing the Change Agent Essentials for all your changes, and challenging anyone within your buffer to do the same.

You can create a celebration buffer and celebrate, early and often, all that you and your team are accomplishing.

You can welcome volunteers from other parts of the organization, community, nation or world, to join you and your corps of change agents. If you do, those under your authority will likely work hard for you and treasure your example and protection. Together, I'm confident you'll achieve wonderful and powerful things.

FROM POWERFUL TO TRANSCENDENT

I can speak with some authority on the effectiveness of creating an island of driving change, even amidst a sea of driving people. I've learned that one person using the Change Agent Essentials is powerful—and a group using the Change Agent Essentials is transcendent.

The Guiding Coalition at Puget Sound Naval Shipyard ran for seven years staffed by less than one full-time employee and funded from the organizational equivalent of the "change found beneath the couch cushions." Yet, at its height, it had over 200 volunteers. Those volunteers agreed to additional work, on top of their regular full-time commitments, to create wonderful, powerful change for the organization they loved.

The list of their wins—their observable, wonderful changes—was long and varied. The Guiding Coalition's changes impacted their organization immediately and other similar organizations soon after. You can create that sort of lasting, powerful change if only you'll try.

POWERFUL ENERGY HIDDEN IN PLAIN SIGHT

As someone who has worked in the nuclear power industry, I'm not surprised to observe seemingly small things that contain enormous power. Applying the Change Agent Essentials is similar to harnessing the enormous power of the invisible atom.

The Change Agent Essentials are the mechanisms through which a change agent unlocks and harnesses the immense power in ourselves, other individuals, and organizations—power that until now has been hiding in plain sight.

Throughout history, some great people have harnessed this power; Lewis & Clark, Rickover, Roosevelt, Wałęsa. We tell stories about their successes.

Some authors like Kotter, Schein, and Covey have described these mechanisms and explained them in their own ways.

In this book, I've tried to move us all one more step down the change path by distilling the behaviors that anyone, anywhere, could apply to begin their change today.

So, if you think you don't have enough people to create your change, try the Change Agent Essentials and you'll find a wealth of volunteers you probably overlooked before.

If you think you don't have enough time to create your change, try the Change Agent Essentials and you'll find more time that you expected.

If you think you don't have the budget to create your change, try the Change Agent Essentials, and you'll figure out how to do what you can, with what you have, where you are. You'll find money in the least expected places—or you may even find you never needed the money you thought you did.

You might not believe it until you try it. I don't blame you. I'll just challenge you to lead with the Change Agent Essentials anyway.

Do what you can, with what you have, where you are.

Why not try?

PARTING WAYS

We must part ways now, but I'm confident you are ready to go forward alone, equipped well with the Change Agent Essentials. You may be setting out on your own after we part, but if you use the Change Agent Essentials, you won't be alone for long. As you lead, others will follow.

I look forward to celebrating with you and the change agents you've inspired. We shall meet again at the pinnacle of your change and admire all that you've accomplished.

Will you start today? I hope you do.

Journey forward, my friend. God bless you. Safe travels!

Appendices

• • •

CHANGE AGENT ACTION TEMPLATES

"Nothing so sharpens the thought process as writing down one's arguments. Weaknesses overlooked in oral discussion become painfully obvious on the written page."

— ADMIRAL H. G. RICKOVER

Included on the following pages are two types of Change Agent Action Templates, one for implementing the Change Agent Essentials via driving change and one for shifting a change from driving people to driving change.

Use the Change Agent Essentials template to design your change plan. I've included a blank template and an example template filled in with the playground project details.

Use the How to Shift template to describe the change situation and to craft action to move it from driving people to driving change. Once you've achieved the shift, feel free to create a new Change Agent Essentials template for your change.

I've included an example Change Agent Essentials template filled with the playground information. And, I've included an example How to Shift template, using Change Algebra.

As you study the templates, notice that they look like a regular sheet of paper. Feel free to create your own Change Agent Action Plan on any piece of paper.

CHANGE AGENT ACTION PLAN: CHANGE AGENT ESSENTIALS TEMPLATE

Title of the Change: *a few words to describe the change*

Current State: *Who and what supports your change today?*

Obstacles & Excuses: *Who or what is stopping you? Who or what are you waiting for? What are your excuses?*

Concrete Goal: *By <date> <who> will <see, feel, taste, touch, experience, or know> <what> <where>.*

Settlers: *(current, missing, past, downstream)*
What are their names, roles, or functions? How many settlers are there?

Change Boundaries: *(now and future)*
Now: What is the boundary of your goal now?
Future: What is the boundary of your future goal?

Assumptions: *What assumptions are people making about you? What assumptions are you making about others or the change? How will you challenge the assumptions?*

Sustainment: *What sustains your change?*
(List partners, funds, authority, change buffers or system changes.)

Try: *What will you do today, with what you have, where you are, to accelerate your change?*

Change Buffers: *(personal, leadership, policy, and celebration)*
What will protect your change until the status quo shifts?

CHANGE AGENT ACTION PLAN: HOW TO SHIFT TEMPLATE

Title of the Change: *a few words to describe the change*

Current State: *Who is driving the change? (Be specific.)*
Who are they driving? (Be specific.)
How are they driving people?
(Examples: issuing policies, sending enforcers, rewarding or punishing behavior)

Concrete Goal: *Is there a concrete goal? If so, write it down.*
If not, what do you think it might be?

Costs: *What are the costs (people, time, results)?*
Include numerical costs, even as estimates, to scope the costs.

Measure the Whirlpool:
How much of your time each week does the change drain?
How much of other people's time does the change drain?
Include numbers, even as estimates, whenever possible.

Corpse Assessment: *Is the change alive (i.e., has the potential to create the results desired), or is it a change corpse?*
Describe how you know.

Assumptions: *What assumptions are people making about you? What assumptions are you making about others? How will you challenge the assumptions?*

Try: *What will you do today, with what you have, where you are, to shift your tactics toward driving change and results?*

EXAMPLE

CHANGE AGENT ACTION PLAN: CHANGE AGENT ESSENTIALS TEMPLATE

Title of the Change: *The playground project*

Current State: *We have energized parents, friends who are special education teachers; and we know some of the people in local government.*

Obstacles & Excuses: *We need connections to the specific government officials. We need to overcome concerns that we are too busy or not connected enough to create the change.*

Concrete Goal: *By as soon as possible, children and adults with special needs in Bremerton, Washington, will experience a beyond accessible playground at Evergreen Rotary Park.*

Settlers: *(current, missing, past, downstream)*
Current: Mayor Patty Lent, Parks Director Wyn Birkenthal, Councilman Greg Wheeler, the Parks Commission, the Rotary Club
Downstream: Local citizens — Children and adults with special needs & their families

Change Boundaries: *(now and future)*
Now: Build and sustain playground at Evergreen Rotary Park.
Future: Rest.

Assumptions: *It will be hard to raise money; try to raise small amounts first and seek larger grants too.*
It will be hard to get other clubs to support a project at the Rotary park; approach them and win their officers to the project.

Sustainment: *Build programs to bring children with special needs to the playground and transfer ownership of the playground and the endowment funds to the City of Bremerton.*

Try:

1. *Meet with the parks director and ask how we can partner.*
2. *Meet with Holly Ridge Executive Director about fundraising.*
3. *Meet with friends and educators to gain more team members.*

Change Buffers: *(personal, leadership, policy, and celebration)*
Personal: Support each other, and gain support from our families.

Leadership: Support from parks director, mayor, city council, and parks commission.

Policy: Change the unwritten rule that clubs only give to projects at their own parks.

Celebration: Celebrate wins at each monthly meeting and hold an anniversary party each year.

EXAMPLE

CHANGE AGENT ACTION PLAN: HOW TO SHIFT TEMPLATE

Title of the Change: *Implement Process P.*

Current State:

Person A is imposing the change.

People in Group B are being driven to change.

Person A issued a policy notice directing everyone in Group B to attend 8 hours of mandatory training on Process P within the next six months.

Those who don't attend will get a non-specified punishment.

Enforcer E will track compliance with this directive.

Concrete Goal: *By six months from now, confirm people in Group B have complied with the order to attend training.*

Costs: *People Costs: X people were already using Process P before the order. After they are forced to go to the 8 hour training, several get frustrated and stop following Process P. Time Costs: 8X hours invested in training. Checks on actual implementation of Process P won't start until after enforcement of training, so results costs are the loss of the benefit of Process P multiplied by the delay in implementation (six months or more).*

Measure the Whirlpool: *Weekly one-hour meetings are held by Enforcer E to track compliance.*

# of attendees multiplied by # of weeks the meeting is held = time drained just to status progress, not to implement Process P.

Corpse Assessment: *Dead. There is no actual punishment for not implementing Process P. Even if compliance with attending the training is high, which it rarely* is in these types of change, that doesn't mean anyone has implemented Process P. Experience suggests that by the time the six months of tracking the change are done, the organizational energy of Person A and Enforcer E will be exhausted and the change will die without implementation of Process P. None of this is a reflection of the merits of Process P. Instead, it is an indictment of the method to implement Process P.

Assumptions: If people in Group B attend the training, they will implement Process P. There aren't any other processes or forces that would stop people, once they know about Process P from implementing it.

Test: Ask people in Group B what keeps them from implementing Process P. People won't implement Process P unless forced to implement it.

Test: Ask who in Group B was following Process P before the order. Ask them why they implemented it without being ordered.

Try:

1. Contact Enforcer E to learn more about why Process P should be implemented and how ordering all the people of Group B to attend training was chosen as the way to implement the change.

2. Ask around in Group B to find someone who implemented Process P either before the training or after the training to understand why they chose to implement it and what obstacles they had to overcome.

3. Read through *Analyzing Performance Problems* by Robert F. Mager and Peter Pipe for other ideas of what to do or what to look for to help people choose to implement Process P.

GLOSSARY

"...[W]e are searching for the power inherent in simply
naming things, for that which we cannot name is lost to
us, and that which we can name is coaxed into life."

— GREGG LEVOY

Celebration Buffer — A commitment to frequently notice, define, and celebrate wins related to your change.

Change Agent Essential — A recommendation for action based on experience and results in similar situations; a heuristic.

Change Algebra — A description of a change story using variables to substitute for specific people, change, and organizations.

Change Boundaries — The limits of your change, both now and in the future.

Change Buffer — Explicit, different thoughts, behaviors, or policies that allow the change agents and the change to vary from the status-quo people and environment.

Change Corpses – Changes that continue after the life has gone out of them.

Change Paths – Graph comparing driving people to driving change, on an axis of energy to drive the implementation versus distance toward the goal.

Change Scars – The psychological vestiges of bad past change efforts that manifest as physical and emotional reactions to new change.

Concrete Goal – Change attributes summarized into one statement that closely follows the pattern:

By <date>, <who> will...

<see, feel, touch, taste, hear, experience, or know>

<what> <where>.

Driving Change – Choosing a change for yourself and clearing the obstacles for others to choose the change too.

Driving People – Using some form of coercion (e.g., orders, fear of negative consequences, removal or application of positive consequences) to compel others to change.

Friendship Buffer - The person or persons you turn to on challenging days to steel your will and give your comfort and strength to continue your change journey.

Leadership Buffer – The protective wing that a leader stretches out to shelter the people who work with them.

Mindset Buffer — A personal commitment to act on your change regardless of the reaction of the people or environment around it.

Personal Buffer — A buffer you can create and maintain independent of the organization related to your change.

Policy Buffer — A deliberate change to a policy that permits you and your change to be different from the status quo.

Settlers - The people who "live on the land" of your change, whose lives will be impacted by it. Settler types include: current, missing, past, and downstream.

Appendix 3

•   •   •

SUGGESTED READINGS

"The only people who achieve much are those who want knowledge so badly that they seek it while the conditions are still unfavorable. Favorable conditions never come."

— *C.S. Lewis*

Your change agent journey has only just begun. This book contains only the essentials to get you started. If you want to move from change novice to apprentice, journeyman, or master, you'll have to fuel yourself with new knowledge and skills. I've included a small list of the authors, thinkers, and practitioners that fuel me. Feel free to use their writings and presentations to fuel you too. You can also search through the 600+ posts at my blog engine-for-change.com or watch my library of keynote videos at www.youtube.com/c/AprilKMills.

FUEL FOR PERSONAL ENERGY & STRENGTH

I recommend combining *StrengthsFinder 2.0* by Tom Rath with the work of Marcus Buckingham, specifically his *Trombone Player Wanted* video. They are better when consumed together, a sort of chocolate-covered strawberry of self-awareness.

FUEL FOR ACCELERATING ORGANIZATIONS

I recommend the works of John Kotter. I would start with his updated eight-step process, which can be found on his website: kotterinternational.com. Follow that up with Kotter's 2014 book *Accelerate*, and the 2016 fable version, *That's Not How We Do It Here!*

FUEL FOR IMPLEMENTING LARGE CHANGE

I recommend the work of Andrea Shapiro: her two books *Creating Contagious Commitment* and *Contagious Commitment at Work*, plus her *Change, Action, and Dialogue Workshop*. If *Everyone is a Change Agent* is Step 1, Andrea's work is Step 2.

FUEL FOR INTERACTING WITH SETTLERS

I recommend the works of Edgar Schein. I would start by reading his recent books, *Humble Inquiry* and *Helping*. Reading the books armed with your new awareness of driving change, you'll find Schein provides enhancements to your change capabilities by putting *helping* and *inquiry* methods into frames that allow you and the people you are engaging to succeed together.

FUEL FOR CHALLENGING ASSUMPTIONS

I recommend the fantastic, practical *Discussing the Undiscussable* by William Noonan. His book and accompanying DVD are a great way to engage a group in conversation about their typical defensive routines during the small and large conflicts that often arise.

FUEL FOR CREATING MORE LEADERS

People with authority who are struggling to see how they can share their authority with others should study David Marquet's *Turn the Ship Around!*. His leader-leader methods can help anyone and any organization shift toward driving change fast.

FUEL FOR ACCESSIBLE PLAYGROUNDS

If you want to learn more about our playground project or see for yourself the joy that accessible play brings to a community, I encourage you to visit Evergreen Rotary Park in Bremerton, Washington, follow the Bremerton Beyond Accessible Play's Facebook page, or watch this fantastic video put together by Cascade DAFO. If you want to see me cry when we received the Bennett Memorial Scholarship Fund donation, watch the short video at http://tinyurl.com/TheLast30K.

Bremerton Beyond Accessible Play on Facebook:

https://www.facebook.com/BeyondAccessiblePlay/

Cascade DAFO video: http://tinyurl.com/BeyondAccessiblePlay

FUEL FOR EVEN MORE SITUATIONS

For a larger list of the authors and books that have influenced my change agent journey, check out my Book Fuel list at: engine-for-change.com/weblog/book-fuel/

Appendix 4

• • •

REFERENCES AND ENDNOTES

Ackoff, Russell. 1978. *The Art of Problem Solving*. New York: John Wiley & Sons.

Andrews, Robert. 2003. *The New Penguin Dictionary of Modern Quotations*. New York: Penguin.

Featured online at http://tinyurl.com/jl72hvz. Contains the Lech Wałęsa quote attributed to an article in *Newsweek*, 27 November 1989. (accessed 22 July 2016)

Appelo, Jurgen. 2012. *How to Change the World: Change Management 3.0*. Rotterdam, the Netherlands: Jojo Ventures BV.

Argyris, Chris. May-June 1991. "Teaching Smart People How to Learn" in *Harvard Business Review*. Boston: Harvard Business Publishing.

Buckingham, Marcus. 2007. *Trombone Player Wanted*. The Marcus Buckingham Company.

Carroll, Lewis. 1945. *Alice's Adventure in Wonderland and Through the Looking-Glass*. Racine, Wisconsin: Whitman Publishing Company.

Collins, Jim. 2001. *Good to Great*. New York: Harper Collins.

Covey, Stephen M.R. 2006. *The Speed of Trust*. New York: Free Press.

Covey, Stephen R. 1994. *First Things First*. New York: Simon & Schuster.

Feynman, Richard. 1974. Caltech Commencement Address. (accessed 10 July 2016) http://calteches.library.caltech.edu/51/2/CargoCult.htm

Goldratt, Eliyahu M. 2008. *The Choice*. Great Barrington, Mass.: North River Press.

Kotter, John. 2014. *Accelerate: Building Strategic Agility for a Faster-Moving World*. Boston: Harvard Business Review Press.

--------. 1996. *Leading Change*. Boston: Harvard Business School Press.

--------. 2016. "The 8-Step Process for Leading Change". Kotter International. (accessed 15 July 2016) http://www.kotterinternational.com/the-8-step-process-for-leading-change/

Kotter, John and Holger Rathgeber. 2016. *That's Now How We Do It Here! A Story about How Organizations Rise and Fall—and Can Rise Again*. New York: Portfolio/Penguin.

Leadership Kitsap. http://www.leadershipkitsap.org/

Lech Wałęsa Institute Foundation. 2016. (accessed 22 July 2016) http://www.ilw.org.pl/en/founder/biography

Levoy, Gregg. 1997. *Callings: Finding and Following an Authentic Life*. New York: Three Rivers Press.

Lewis, C.S. 2001. *The Weight of Glory: And Other Addresses*. San Francisco: HarperSanFrancisco.

Lucas, Kalli. 2007. History of Washington County, Virginia Mills. (accessed 22 July 2016) http://www.millsofwashingtoncounty.com

Mager, Robert F. and Peter Pipe. 1997. *Analyzing Performance Problems*. Atlanta: The Center for Effective Performance.

Malotaux, Niels. 2015. (accessed 22 July 2016) http://www.malotaux.nl

The quote, "Beware the stakeholder..." was quoted to the author in conversation and email by Mr. Malotaux. For more of his Malotaux Mantras, visit http://www.malotaux.eu/?id=mantras.

Marquet, L. David 2012. *Turn the Ship Around!* New York: Portfolio/Penguin.

Maxwell, John C.. 2002. *Thinking for a Change: 11 Ways Highly Successful People Approach Life and Work*. New York: Warner Business Books.

Mills, April K. 2016. Engine-for-Change blog posts. http://engine-for-change.com

--------. 2011. *The Path to Success: How to Make Any Implementation Successful*. 2011 Theory of Constraints International Certification Organization (TOCICO) Conference. New York. http://tinyurl.com/2011TOCICO-Mills

-------- . 2015. *Driving Change*. Gdansk, Poland. http://tinyurl.com/DrivingChange-Gdansk2016

-------- . Videos. https://www.youtube.com/c/AprilKMills

Morris, Edmund. 1979. *The Rise of Theodore Roosevelt*. New York: Coward, McCann & Geoghegan.

Neuberger, Richard L.. 1951. *The Lewis and Clark Expedition*. New York: Random House.

Noonan, William R.. 2007. *Discussing the Undiscussable: A Guide to Overcoming Defensive Routines in the Workplace*. San Francisco: Jossey-Bass.

Parkinson, C. Northcote. 1957. *Parkinson's Law and Other Studies in Administration*. Cambridge, Mass.: The Riverside Press.

Pfeffer, Jeffrey and Sutton, Robert I. 2000. *The Knowing-Doing Gap: How Smart Companies Turn Knowledge Into Action*. Boston: Harvard Business School Press.

Pirsig, Robert M. 1974. *Zen and the Art of Motorcycle Maintenance: An Inquiry Into Values*. New York: William Morrow and Company.

Rath, Tom. 2007. *StrengthsFinder2.0*. New York: Gallup Press.

Rickover, H. G.. January 28, 1982. "Economics of Defense Policy" in *Hearing Before the Joint Economic Committee of the Ninety-Seventh Congress of the United States*. Washington, DC: U.S. Government Printing Office.

An online version of the testimony was available to review as of 22 July 2016 at the following link:
http://tinyurl.com/rickovercongress1982

Rockwell, Theodore. 1992. *The Rickover Effect: How One Man Made a Difference.* Lincoln, Nebraska: Naval Institute Press.

Schein, Edgar H.. 2009. *Helping: How to Offer, Give and Receive Help.* San Francisco: Berrett-Koehler Publishers.

--------. 2013. *Humble Inquiry: The Gentle Art of Asking Instead of Telling.* Oakland, California: Berrett-Koehler Publishers.

Shapiro, Andrea. 2013. *Change, Dialogue, and Action Workshop.* Hillsborough, North Carolina: Strategy Perspective.

--------. 2016. *Contagious Commitment at Work: Applying the Tipping Point to Organizational Change.* Hillsborough, North Carolina: Strategy Perspective.

--------. 2003. *Creating Contagious Commitment: Applying the Tipping Point to Organizational Change.* Hillsborough, North Carolina: Strategy Perspective.

United States Navy Correspondence Manual, SECNAVINST 5216.5, (Accessed 20 July 2016) http://www.jag.navy.mil/distrib/instructions/SECNAVINST5216.5Navy CorrespondenceManual.pdf

Wałęsa, Lech. 21 May 2000. *Middlebury College Commencement Address.* (accessed 22 July 2016) http://www.middlebury.edu/newsroom/commencement/2000

Wikipedia.org, "Cargo cult" (accessed 6 July 2016) https://en.wikipedia.org/wiki/Cargo_cult

Wikipedia.org, "Cobra effect" (accessed 18 July 2016)
https://en.wikipedia.org/wiki/Cobra_effect

Wikipedia.org, "Lech Wałęsa" (accessed 10 July 2016)
https://en.wikipedia.org/wiki/Lech_Wałęsa

Wikipedia.org, "Student Syndrome" (access 18 August 2016)
https://en.wikipedia.org/wiki/Student_syndrome

Wikipedia.org, "Theory of Constraints" (accessed 10 July 2016)
https://en.wikipedia.org/wiki/Theory_of_Constraints

Wikipedia.org, "Traffic Light Tree." (accessed 20 July 2016)
https://en.wikipedia.org/wiki/Traffic_Light_Tree

Wikiquote.org, "Henry David Thoreau." (accessed 20 July 2016)
https://en.wikiquote.org/wiki/Henry_David_Thoreau

Wikiquote.org, "Hyman G. Rickover" (accessed 14 July 2016)
https://en.wikiquote.org/wiki/Hyman_G._Rickover

The quote "More that rules.." comes from a speech Admiral Rickover delivered to the U.S. Naval Postgraduate School on 16 March 1954.

Wikiquote.org, "Johann Wolfgang von Goethe" (accessed 20 July 2016)
https://en.wikiquote.org/wiki/Johann_Wolfgang_von_Goethe

The quote, "…[M]isunderstandings…" is reported to have come from his 1774 book, *The Sorrows of Young Werther.*

Wikiquote.org, "Marianne Williamson" (accessed 16 July 2016).
https://en.wikiquote.org/wiki/Marianne_Williamson

The quote, "Our deepest fear..." is reported to have come from
her 1992 book, *A Return to Love: Reflections on the Principles of "A
Course in Miracles."* published by HarperCollins.

Wikiquote.org, "William Clark (explorer)" (accessed 22 July 2016)
https://en.wikiquote.org/wiki/William_Clark_(explorer)

ABOUT THE AUTHOR

April K. Mills is a devoted student and practitioner of the art of change. *Everyone is a Change Agent* is her first book.

Her personal mission is to give the world words that can ignite actions that solve problems, seize opportunities, and enrich lives.

A native of Amery, Wisconsin, she studied Engineering Mechanics at the University of Wisconsin—Madison and was the first in her family to graduate from college.

After graduation, April and her biochemist-turned-lawyer husband, Matt, moved to Bremerton, Washington. There, for nearly 14 years, she worked proudly as a civilian for the U.S. Navy at Puget Sound Naval Shipyard and Intermediate Maintenance Facility (PSNS & IMF). The Navy and the Bremerton community nurtured April's love of change and lit a fire in her to make a positive difference in the world.

In 2014, April joined Intel Corporation as a Leadership Engineer and Change Coach, a custom position designed to bring her practical, cutting-edge ideas about change to Intel's global workforce.

Since 2009 April has blogged at Engine for Change (engine-for-change.com), her website dedicated to sharing stories of driving change and the change agent essentials.

April lives in Cornelius, Oregon, with her husband and their four children, large black lab, and two cats. She rarely has free time, but when she does, she loves to relax with a great book or drive with her husband and kids to their next adventure—usually at a national park or a stop along the Lewis and Clark expedition route.

Contact April through her blog at engine-for-change.com, on Twitter at @engineforchange or via email at april@engine-for-change.com.

ABOUT THE ILLUSTRATOR

An Oregon native, self-proclaimed Visual Storyteller Sarah Moyle currently lives in Beaverton Oregon, with her husband, son, two cats and two dogs. Though art has always been a passion for Sarah, she didn't formally study art in school because she felt like she needed to get a "real job." After a couple of years at Intel Corporation, she created her own job, marrying art with industry to explain complicated subjects, facilitate discussions, and share her talent for drawing with the corporate world.

Sarah's passions lie around not only creating art herself, but bringing art into others' lives by drawing, speaking about drawing, and teaching workshops. She looks forward to sharing her love of analog creation with her children as they grow. A rabid entertainer and Halloween enthusiast, Sarah's house is an annual (and spooky) art project all its own. To see more of Sarah's creations, visit her website at www.sarahmoyle.com.

Made in the USA
Lexington, KY
23 November 2019

57506274R00114